Becoming
IN-LIGHTENED

Clearing the Path to Spirituality

DENISE GANULIN

Dega Publishing

This book is published by
Dega Publishing
11956 Bernardo Plaza Dr. #312
San Diego, CA 92128

CONTENTS

Thank You for Buying

Becoming
IN-LIGHTENED

I am so glad you decided to buy my book! As my gift to you for buying my book, I have decided to offer you a free journal to help you get started and guide you along the way. Just visit my website, <u>DeniseGanulin. com,</u> for more details and to get your free journal today. If you have any questions, you can email me there as well.

I wish you a joyful and blessed journey on your path to becoming IN~lightened.

~Denise Ganulin

INTRODUCTION

When my daughter, Holland, passed away in 2013, I felt like the entire world had crashed down on top of me. I didn't think that I would ever be able to recover from it. Several years before my daughter died, a good friend of hers was killed in a bus accident. One day, I ran into her father, and said to him, "I can't imagine what you are going through."

His response was, "No, you can't."

At the time, I actually thought he was being rude. But then, when my daughter (and only child) died, I knew exactly what he meant. On top of every other hurt in my life, that was one too many and of a magnitude that I never thought existed. I felt broken and unmendable. I'd had many other "disappointments" in my life that impacted my development and outlook on everything. It was easy for me to feel like a victim of life. Both my parents were gone, and now my only child. I had plenty of childhood experiences that formed my opinions of myself and my world, several failed relationships over the years, and many things that just didn't go the way

I wanted. I guess you could say that, like most of us, I have had my share of taking blows.

Interestingly, my daughter and I shared a longing and desire to know about Spirituality, God, and the Universe. We read books and talked for hours and hours about the "other side" and what this life was all about. We somehow knew that this life was a journey to find that sweet sacred space and that there was no other way. And yet, when Holland died, all of what we learned and thought we knew, flew out the window for me.

Six months after she died, I went away for a long month all by myself with dozens of self-help books on grief, having a positive attitude, and Spirituality. I could barely get through those books, but I kept reading because somehow, I knew that the key to my freedom was raising my consciousness and connecting with that spiritual part that lies in each of us to find the peace I was seeking. It certainly wasn't in food, alcohol, or drugs, all of which I tried. I was full of hurt, resentment, questions, anger, "why me," and self-pity. I couldn't seem to find any answers that satisfied me.

Everyone was talking about becoming "enlightened," and I thought that was what I wanted and needed to get me through. I just couldn't see how to do it. I was stuck, frozen even. In searching, what I found was that I was so heavy inside with the many boulders I had collected with all that had happened over the years of my life, that I couldn't get to that spiritual place.

What I learned was that what I needed was to lighten my load *inside* to make room for that place that the Universe was trying to fill. It was easy to blame God or the Universe, or whatever else I could blame for my misfortunes, but that only made me feel heavier. For me to move forward with my life, I needed to clean house and open my heart. I found that when I turned away from anything spiritual, that was when I needed it most.

I also learned that in order to connect with Spirit and become enlightened, I first had to deal with all that I was carrying around and become IN-lightened. And from that journey, this book was born.

- As I share my journey with you, you will learn about IN-lightenment and exactly what that means.
- You will discover the steps you need to achieve healing and peace no matter what losses, traumas, and wounds you have experienced in your life so far.
- As you follow the steps to IN-lightenment, you, too, will be able to lighten yourself *inside* by crushing and removing the many boulders that you have collected through the years.
- And you will see how to avoid and prevent new boulders from ever weighing you down again.

To help you get started, there is a free journal waiting for you on my website: DeniseGanulin.com, If you have any questions, you can email me there as well.

I wish you many blessings and abundant
love on your magnificent journey.

~Denise Ganulin

CHAPTER 1

What If?

What if I told you that I think all the boulders that weigh us down inside come from loss? Loss of a loved one, loss of health, loss of money, loss of a job, loss of our self-esteem and confidence, loss of purpose, loss of our youth, loss of control, power, and importance, loss of a career, loss of our physical looks, hair, eyesight, hearing … You name it, and throughout our lives, we pile up one loss after the other. It happens to all of us in some form or another. The only thing I can remember ever losing that felt good was weight!! And that really didn't make up for any of the other losses I had … Not even close.

Let's start with the obvious premise that we all have mounds of hurts, disappointments, wounds, traumas, and less than wonderful experiences in our lives, beginning with childhood when we are most vulnerable. It happens to all of us, no matter what our color, race, religion, sexual orientation, or any other "category" we may fit into. What we all have in common is that we're the same inside as *souls*, but we are all affected by what happens to us as *humans*. These experiences shape us. They stay with us. They infect us and hold us back. They generate all kinds of negative feelings that cause one "spiritual oil spill" after another. Some of us might process these experiences and feelings more profoundly or more intensely than others, but we all still try to deal with them in some way. When we can't find a resolution, we stuff them all down to where we don't have to deal with them or think about them. Or we lament our losses in a way that keeps us from enjoying any part of our lives at all. Like a trash can that is getting full, we then stand on it to squash it down even further, trying to make it all fit in the can.

If the trash can in our kitchen gets full, we just empty it and start over. But for ourselves, we stuff it down and keep it. We remember it. We carry it around with us. We hold on to it. That becomes our baggage, and that baggage becomes who we are (or who we *think* we are). It becomes our identity. We all might as well have a big red wagon to pull behind us that holds all that stuff ... but instead, we push it down inside, cram it in, hide it, cover it up, and yet, like the boulders they are, they stay hard and strong. They impact our reactions and decision-making. They make us not trust, fill our heads with negative thoughts, and fill our hearts with negative emotions. This can lead to depression, anxiety, and self-pity.

Some might tell you to "fake it till you make it." What does that really mean? Does it mean we should pretend and ignore those feelings? Even if we could pretend, those feelings, issues, and disappointments keep piling up like a growth that gets so big we just can't ignore it one more minute.

So, what if the Universe is trying to fill us with peace, joy, love, and everything wonderful? Where would we put it if we are so full of all the other negative stuff, there is no room left? What if these gifts are being offered to us daily, hourly even? We wouldn't even notice anymore. We would be too busy crying about the past, worrying about the future, and spending all of our energy just trying to get through the day.

If you are pushing a shopping cart and it's practically full, you would only have room left for the things you *think* you need or want most, like comforting junk food when your body might be starving for fruits and veggies. Soon, you get used to eating junk, and you don't even know what it feels like to feel healthy, so you think about it less and less and then adjust to this way of feeling as though it's the way it's supposed to be. Then our bodies get sick, and we don't understand why. And that result is just another boulder to put in our trash cans. And that means more that we can lament over and feel bad about. We adjust and get used to the pain and think that's just how it is.

But what if the Universe is trying to give us gifts? And what if the Universe offers only good? What brings people to seek out Spirit/God? Many times, it's the last place they turn to after a big trauma or bad luck when they feel they have run out of options. Seeking God/the Universe is a last resort because the way we are handling things is just not working. And many of us secretly hold God responsible for our misfortunes. But the Universe/God does not give us our problems and traumas. No. Those just happen, as we will see and understand more as we explore later chapters. Problems and traumas, hurts and disappointments just happen; to all of us. The Universe tries to get our attention during the reaction phase of the trauma. In other words, how we react to what happens to us is where the Universe can and will help if we just listen to the call.

What if the reason we keep having misfortunes is due to the way we react to those misfortunes? What if we need a different direction? We have options after the trauma or loss, and those options on how to respond are the gifts from the Universe. If we don't exercise those options (gifts), we very well may create more of the same misfortunes and more boulders. And we do. We become so bogged down and closed that we stop seeing another way. What if we could not only stop creating new boulders, but we could actually remove those old boulders from our overflowing loads?

Since you are reading this book, chances are you're in this spiritual bog, and you're searching for a way out like I was. After my daughter died, I sank to the lowest point of my life. I thought about it from the first minute I opened my eyes (if I had gotten any sleep at all), and it hung over me for the entire day. I felt like one of those little wind-up toys that walks into a wall and then turns and keeps on going until it hits another wall, and this just continues until it runs out of juice. That wind-up toy actually went nowhere. I found that I was handling all my losses the same way and kept hitting the same wall over and over. Sound familiar?

What if everything that happens brings us closer to where we need to be, especially trauma, death, grief, and illness? What if every experience is for the purpose of our spiritual growth? Without any problems in life, we would never have an opportunity to grow, learn, adapt, or mature. If we knew that, then how would we look at those experiences? We think others are having it better than we are, but famous, wealthy people also get divorced, have grief, and know illness. If they were all so happy, they wouldn't need drugs, booze, or suicide to deal with their problems. Would we really want to be them?? Even they are still empty of something. What is that something?? What if it's God?

I want to clarify what I mean when I refer to God. I use God, Spirit, Light, and the Universe interchangeably to address Spirituality. I'm not talking about religion. There are thousands of religions, and they all think they have the one special secret. I can't tell you how many different religions I have tried, only to come away asking myself: "What if it's more general and available to all of us no matter what religion we are following?"

What if the Universe is pure Spirit, all around us and inside us? It's within us, always. We are born with it. It never leaves us, but rather we leave it. We step out of it. We blame it. We keep all the boulders of disappointment and hurt, and soon there is no room for Spirit or Spirituality. With every boulder, that Spirit is covered, buried even, until we can't see it anymore. It's still there, but we are no longer aware of it. We try to "handle" our problems as we try to control everything around us. We can't. That frustration causes us to try to hold on tighter.

One of my daughter's favorite sayings was, "Just loosen your grip!" What she was saying was to let go. Let go of all that old junk and make room for Spirit. My experience tells me that when we are spiraling out of control, we will grab on and try to control anything we can. I've done it many times … and it never helped! So how can we get on the path to Spirituality and IN-lightenment? How can we feel peace inside?

What if you could wake up each day with no memory of the past? What if you could start new each day with a fresh slate and *know* that you will be filled with all you need and, in fact, already *are*, all you need to be? What if we didn't think a soul was just something we have, but rather we just *are* soul? And what if that soul is light … Light, as in brightness, and light, as in a feather. How would that feel?

I see this process of filling up with boulders throughout our lives like a day that turns into night. First, the day is bright and sunny, then as negative things happen, the day becomes clouded, or dusky, gradually until finally, it is pitch dark. But even in the pitch dark of night, we can look out and see stars shining. Even the darkest night will end, and the sun will rise. The light is always there; we just need to turn around (rotate) like the earth until we are in the sun again by letting go of all the negative stuff and making room for the light … the spiritual light. Even if your trash can can't hold another boulder, there will still be little areas where the boulders don't touch or fit together perfectly. Those are the areas for your stars of light. And that light never leaves us.

What if it doesn't matter what religion I am? The light is there for me and everyone else. I can't ever take another's light. There is an unlimited supply for all. And since it doesn't matter what religion I may be, or what religion anyone may be, we would all have this light to share, and that alone would give us all a common bond. And what if that spiritual light represents one presence and one power that is always available to everyone, and we don't have to do anything special to have it (like giving money, going to confession, wearing something special, or performing rituals just allowed for one religious group)?

What if everything that happens to us is an opportunity for spiritual awakening, growth, elevation, and realization? Additionally, what if the more intense the situation we are facing, the higher we could elevate and grow? What if we just stopped looking for answers to why and accept that everything that happens is for our highest good? Even if it's not obvious at the moment, it's still working for us. Some would call this faith. Still, even though it's there, we have to seek it. We have to find it. And as a child, wasn't it more rewarding to find that easter egg that was hidden instead of the ones that were right out in the open? When we are at our lowest and need the light the most, that's when we can't seem to find it. And that's when we need to look harder because it's always there waiting for us. We are the ones that turn away from it.

In order to understand the path to Spirituality—true Spirituality—we need to understand how our trash cans fill up, how we can manage our spiritual oil spills, and how to cleanse them on our journey to the light, but it starts by understanding how it all begins.

CHAPTER 2

In the Beginning

*W*hen we are in the womb, we have everything we need. We don't worry about anything. We get the nourishment we need, the nutrients we need, and everything we require to grow and flourish. All we have to do is receive the goods and just *be*. Once we are ready, we come into the world as perfect beings, created in the image and likeness of God, if you will. Perfect and whole. Identical. We are all the same pure spiritual beings. It doesn't matter if we are born Caucasian in California, Black in Alabama, Asian in China, Muslim in Iran, or Indian in India. Yes, we might have different exteriors, but if you peel away our skin and outer covering, are we not all exactly the same if you put us in an x-ray machine? We have the same body parts, organs, and bones. We all bleed red when we are cut. Our laboratory test ranges are the same no matter what we look like or where we come from. We are all susceptible to the same diseases. So, the only thing that differentiates us is the outer coating. That, in itself, seems to be a reason for us to hate each other ... just because *they* don't look like *us*. But the similarities are far greater than that *one* difference ... the difference of appearance.

If we really are soul, and that soul is the same as all souls, then why are we so influenced by the outer coating? I wonder what it would be like to communicate with others on that soul level? All members of the same group. Just think what a common bond that would be! But it seems to go by the wayside shortly after birth.

In all walks of life, babies start out the same. They have the same basic needs. They cry when they are hungry. They live in the moment. They feel pure joy. They can play with a toy without time constraints. They can cry for food, then let it go and laugh about something else, leaving that other moment in the past. They don't keep crying about the feeding they had to wait for. They actually have no judgment or anger on that. And there is no worry about the next time they might be hungry. They are just happy to *be* in the now.

When a new baby is born, to them, everything outside of themselves is also new. They want to see everything, touch everything, experience everything. They seem to have no fear of anything. They learn to walk, and they fall down over and over again. Do they lay there thinking it's not worth walking anymore? No! They get up and walk, again and again, with the same enthusiasm they had the first time. Then one day, they take off running.

Why is it, then, that we lose that determination and enthusiasm as we grow? We stop trying. We learn to quit. If something doesn't come easy, we give up. We look for constant stimulation outside of ourselves and get further away from "being." A child will laugh over and over at the same thing instead of looking for other things by the minute. We, adults, think we need to constantly stimulate the baby, sing to them, rock them, make faces, and coochie-coo them. And if we are too busy as a parent to "entertain" our baby, we sit them in front of a television so they can get more nonstop stimulation, again, outside of themselves. Could that be the first lesson in looking outside ourselves to be happy?

Then, as a result, we start thinking it's because of others that we are happy or not happy. It's a lesson that teaches us that we are not enough as we are and that we need to look for more. Then when we don't get it, we learn to judge and blame, two of the big spiritual oil spills we will explore in Chapter 3.

We develop the basis for doing instead of being. We can't sit still. We need to be doing something, and as soon as we begin to stop just being and make it all about doing, we begin to collect and hold on to those boulders that we start dragging around. Like what can we *do* to feel better? The answer is to go inside ourselves and just *be* again, but we don't do that. We try to *do* one thing after another. We begin to hold on to the past as we worry about the future. We start trying all kinds of ways to control our world and even the worlds of others.

What began as a pure soul, happy to be in the moment, always in touch with Spirit, somehow changes along the way and becomes the dumping ground for all our negative experiences, or what we start to identify as negative. When we are born, we have no preconceived notions, no self-esteem, no ideas of good and bad, no opinions or biases. But we learn quickly about what our parents think is good or bad, right, or wrong. We learn how to live within the parameters that our parents set up. We learn, accept, and take on their biases, opinions, and rules. Our belief system is being created.

We see and believe that if we please our parents, then we are okay, even if it means no longer being who we really are. We start to take on limiting thoughts and beliefs. We learn early on that we are not good enough, and we take that in. Most of us are not taught that we are perfect beings, full of love, and acceptable just as we are. Instead, we need to be "shown the way" with constant correction from our parents, teachers, coaches, ministers, and everyone we come in contact with as we grow and develop.

And then we are taught that we are different from others, disconnected from others based on the beliefs and biases (yes, and bigotries) of our parents and other adult "authorities." Even some religious leaders teach us that we are born of sin and need salvation. They say if we don't believe this way or that way, we are doomed to hell. We kill in the name of whatever we call God, and we disconnect from other souls as if we all come from different planets with no similarities. We begin to just go through the motions of our lives. Instinctively, we know something is off, but we don't know what it is.

What if what we learn and are taught as children just isn't true? What if God is pure love? What if God is inside of us and all around us all the time, and we can get to that place anytime we want? Didn't Jesus say that "the kingdom of heaven is within"? (Luke 17:21.) I've always wondered why I have to die to know heaven. Oh, and, of course, follow some religious dogma to get my ticket into heaven.

We can find heaven right here and now by seeking the light and being in it. We can lighten ourselves inside. But instead, many of us are not looking inside. We keep trying to control whatever we can control or think we can control on the outside. We turn to addictions of all kinds. We fail, then we give up and wallow in our own self-pity. Not always, and not everyone, but many.

And then there are those who "pretend" that it's all okay, but inside they are collecting the gunk that will load them down later. We try to be what we are not so that people will like us, but we don't like ourselves. How many times have you heard of someone who takes their own life, and you had no idea they were that troubled? They mastered the art of being something they were not, then were not able to live with that. These impressions and behaviors begin as a small child. For some, it's the only way they can survive their environment.

We develop fears, and our actions become ruled by our fears. We develop our egos, which then want to defend our sense of self as we choose our likes and dislikes (many of which come from the adults in our lives) and claim our preferences as if those preferences are us. We become who we are as our egos discover protection methods, all the while making us feel more inadequate than we felt before.

And then we have more spiritual oil spills when our ego steps in with anger, resentment, blame, shame, and more. So just trying to live a life that has been "taught" to us begins the clogging process. It all takes us further away from the silence and peace inside us, and we lose the art of just *being*. I have often wondered if ADHD kids are really just over-stimulated as they are bombarded by sounds and visuals all day long. So much so that they can't stand the quiet anymore … And if they don't comply in school or at home, the quiet timeout is a punishment, so they develop an aversion to the silence … where the light and all its goodness can be found.

And while children are growing, they are instructed to accomplish things … *do* something. Just DO it! They get opinions from adults who are in a place of power as to what is good, bad, right, and wrong. They are made to feel that they must reach for the stars … not for the light, but for the prize. But the prize *is* the light, not the plaque, ribbon, or piece of paper they are taught to go after. And let's not forget how guilt is used to snap us into line if we dare to go in a different direction.

No wonder we are so loaded down.

Maybe we don't have to *do* anything but just *be*. Share love, experiences, ideas, and everything that brings us light. We can neither lose our light nor take it from another. There would be no reason to feel threatened or in danger. Instead of competing, we would be sharing and helping. Instead of beating someone out, we would be traveling *with* them in love and Spirit. The more we give, the more we would get. I find this a very interesting concept!

Right now, I'm troubled by what is happening in this country. I love my country, but somehow, the politicians are more interested in winning than doing what is good and right for our people. There is no light in this or anything about this—just more boulders. And the more they kick up the dust, the more we all feel the trouble. Remember, God is not responsible for any negativity, but we are so mired in it that we have lost our way. We need to find our way back to the beginning. We need to see and respond to situations at the soul level. If everything is divinely ordered and there for us to spiritually grow, then maybe we need a different perspective on our problems. Just a thought!

My experience tells me that I put myself in hell right here by allowing every oil spill in my life to spread out over my soul so that I couldn't even get close to that place I now know exists. It seemed like with every boulder, I was getting further away from the zone of being in the flow. The traumas, wounds, and limiting beliefs became my conditioning and were in the way of me getting back to my pure soul. Every new negative event triggered my memory of negative feelings. I was stuck in a downward spiral.

We all have that sacred space within us, but it gets covered up from the time we are born with all of the boulders that come with every negative reaction, our self-hatred, and feelings of not being good enough as we are. We then act on those negative (and incorrect feelings), making choices that reinforce those thoughts. We continuously seek happiness (in whatever form we think it is). When we can't find it, we medicate ourselves with drugs, alcohol, sex, antidepressants, anti-anxiety medication, food, therapists, television, and anything else that can numb us and give us an escape and a break from our reality. I've tried them all, but none of them gave me the peace I was so desperately seeking.

I had to wonder if the answer was simpler than what I was thinking. What if all I had to do was just take a breath, close my eyes, and go deep inside my soul to my pre-essence where I could reconnect with my wholeness? What if all I really needed was right there, and what if it actually could feel better than any of the other external medications and "remedies" I just mentioned? For me, it started as just a theory. But since nothing else worked, I thought I should look deeper into it. What did I have to lose? I certainly had hit rock bottom. I couldn't see a way up and out, which got me thinking. I knew I didn't want to stay where I was, but I just couldn't see beyond that door that seemed slammed shut right in my face. Every situation was overwhelming and elicited negative feelings with resulting spiritual oil spills. I felt heavy and loaded down.

Imagine a hot air balloon. It wants to go up, but it's too heavy. It cannot go up, no matter how much hot air you keep pumping into it. So, what does the pilot do? He has to start throwing weight out of that basket so that it's light enough to rise. That's just what we have to do. Throw out all that heavy stuff so that we, too, can rise.

Spiritual oil spills are things that gunk up the works for us. We think it's our experiences. That's only partly true. It's more like the feelings we feel and dwell on and won't let go of that come with those experiences. It's our reactions to our misfortunes and situations. I'm talking about:

- Fear
- Anger
- Grief
- Resentment
- Judgment
- Low self-worth/esteem
- Self-pity

Still, there are many other negative feelings not even listed here! We all have years and years of these feelings until not only do we lose faith and step away from any spiritual connection, but we are frozen, and we become completely lost until we don't think a spiritual connection is even possible.

We first must let go of what happened yesterday. We need to keep our slate clean and stop keeping score of our problems, injustices, and disappointments. We need to keep that spiritual part of us open and clear so that we have room to fill it with the most beautiful experiences that can only come from connecting spiritually. We all have a spiritual ladder and the ability to climb it, but we can also fall.

Imagine if oil was on every step of that ladder … it would make it pretty hard to get to the top. We'd be slipping every step of the way. All of our spiritual oil spills keep us from reaching the top of the ladder. We all have these spills. We can continue to deal with them as we have (unsuccessfully), or we can find a new way. In order to find that new way, we first must look at and be able to recognize the spiritual oil spills that we all face.

CHAPTER 3

Spiritual Oil Spills

What exactly do I mean when I say "spiritual oil spills," and what causes them? If we are all born pure soul with a deep connection to Spirit, then what causes us to lose that connection? Can you think of a time when you were a child when an adult inferred that you were a "bad boy" or a "bad girl" for something you did? They made what you did … *you*. Can you remember that sick feeling in your stomach and your embarrassment? Maybe you were sent to your room, and you didn't want to come out. You felt so bad and ashamed if you did think you did something "wrong" or "bad." If you were unfairly or incorrectly called out, you might have felt angry, helpless, and confused.

That might have been the first time you had a spiritual oil spill. You felt less than you did before that incident. Or perhaps your parents were busy, and you "bothered" them, and they dismissed you. You felt insignificant, as though you didn't count. You began to learn that approval was better than disapproval. So you had to figure out how to get that approval, even if it meant "impersonating" whatever or whoever you thought was expected from you to get that "good" rating. ("Don't interrupt," "Children should be seen and not heard," "Do what I tell you," "Because I said so.")

And when you started going to school, the teacher got to determine your rating, and then you had to show them what *they* needed to see to give you that good rating. Then you went to your religious leader and learned what they expected or what they told you God expected. You slowly began the process of losing yourself, questioning yourself, hating yourself. As your ego developed, so did all of the negative emotions that created the boulders that began to fill your soul. That was the same soul that once filled that happy, joyful child, and the result was that the pure soul you were born with slowly faded into the distance.

We try to soothe ourselves, but we cannot. We don't know how. We need our blanket, a special stuffed animal, or anything outside ourselves. My daughter was a great cook. When she died, I lost interest in food, especially the foods she used to prepare. I tried eating to self-soothe, but it didn't work. Then I tried drinking, and although, for the moment, I found it somewhat soothing, the after-effects came with more overwhelming depression. I couldn't find the light. When we are deep in the middle of a spiritual oil spill, we don't feel the light, and we can't seem to find it when we are spilling over with negativity. Whatever experience caused our pain, we try to cover it up with another negative feeling. And these cause bigger spills until we are so heavy that we can't even remember what it was like to be in the light.

The light within our souls becomes unfamiliar to us and a place we have no recollection of ever being and no map of how to get back there. But still, we grow up, and instead of our blanket, we find alcohol, food, drugs, sexual behaviors, and more because we are now unsure of who we are. We have bosses to please, boyfriends or girlfriends to please, but by now, we are in the mode of trying to give others what *they* want. We bend, mold ourselves, and accommodate. We know, in some way, that we are selling out, but we can't stop. It's the way it has been, and we can't see another way. We take on negative behaviors (many in secret) and then feel bad about them.

We now have boulders, and the ball is rolling downhill ... or I should say, the boulders are stacking up. And as they stack up, we accumulate a plethora of negative emotions to draw from, each one resulting in yet another boulder. And even though we feel uncomfortable much of the time within ourselves, those negative emotions are what become familiar to us. How can we stop this cycle before we pass it all down to our children for yet another generation of lost souls?

Let's explore some of the many negative emotions that cause spiritual oil spills. These are all obstacles to happiness and inner peace.

Let me just mention here that I am not an "expert" or a professional psychologist (although I do have a degree in psychology). However, I have lived and experienced what many others have experienced, and it's those experiences that I draw from. I have talked with many people of all ages, from many walks of life, and found that we do go through things in a lot of the same ways. I have a feeling you will be able to relate to much of what I'm talking about. Just like we are all born the same, full of a pure Spirit, we also all fill our cans with what we go through, and as we pile up our boulders, we become all too familiar with these spiritual oil spills.

We all have had different degrees and types of losses, but we all have had losses (or perceived losses), nonetheless. There are so many negative feelings we can have ... way more than positive feelings (which I find interesting in itself!). And after talking to many, many people, I discovered the most common negative emotions are:

Fear	Anger
Resentment	Blame
Vengefulness	Shame/Guilt
Jealousy/Envy	Judgement
Defensiveness	Worry/Anxiety
Disconnection	Despair/Hopelessness

Let's take a closer look at each one.

FEAR

An unpleasant emotion caused by the belief or perception that someone or something is dangerous, likely to cause pain, or a threat.

I think fear may be one of the most intense of the spiritual oil spills. Thousands of years ago, when man first appeared, it seems we were hard-wired with the fight or flight response. There were many dangers. Those dangers caused us to be fearful. Then, once we felt that fear and knew about it, it just kept coming back up. An animal smells fear and reacts to it, and they feel that fear in that moment, but they continue on with their lives when the fearful situation is over. They don't drag it with them throughout their entire lives, agonizing as they remember. *We* do.

Fear holds us back and keeps us heavy. We can't be in a state of fear and be happy or feel *good* emotions at the same time. It's just not possible. Fear consumes us for the time we are feeling it. It leads to self-judgment, self-doubt, embarrassment, anger, anxiety, and resentments (more negative feelings). It is paralyzing and debilitating and can smother us so that we can't feel love or gratitude or any other good feelings that will place us in the light. Fear is one of the biggest holds on our thoughts and behaviors:

"I'm afraid it won't work."

"I'm afraid I'm not good enough."

"I'm afraid I will make a fool of myself."

"I'm afraid they won't like me."

And on and on.

If we are afraid of a "thing," such as being in a small space, we must try and change fear into preference. "I prefer not to be in closed spaces." Just that small change in perception can make such a big difference. If we live in fear of something, like the fear of making a fool of ourselves, then we might never dance, sing, or put ourselves on the line for anything. We will miss some amazing opportunities while being submerged in that fear—no chance of feeling the light or even being able to notice the light in this state. And as a result, we begin to have more spiritual oil spills on top of the fear.

Personally, I struggled for many years with the fear of not being good enough when it came to one of my great passions. I have always loved music. I played the piano, but not all that well. I knew I could change lyrics to any existing song, but I didn't feel like I played an instrument well enough to write original music. I did some writing with other musicians who wrote the music to my lyrics, but I always heard my own music in my head. I didn't act on my talents because I had so much self-doubt, so I made my way in the business world as my music faded into the background. I would still get song ideas, but the self-doubt (fear) would always creep in. I did go into the studio to record some of my songs, but I would never sing them myself. I didn't think I was a good enough singer, and I was afraid of making a fool of myself.

So, I would hire studio singers. My self-doubt prevailed. I was so frozen that I would not and could not bring myself to participate in singer/songwriter events. So, my songs stayed relatively private. But one day, when I was much older, I wrote a sweet spiritual song. I took it to the music director of the spiritual center that I attended at the time. I offered it to her for her to sing. She wrote her own songs and told me that I would have to sing it myself. It was a small center, and I had a friend who encouraged me to step outside of my comfort zone and try it. She heard the song and really liked it. She told me not to let my fear take over. This was a song that needed to be heard.

I think it's interesting that the song was called "Let Go"! I don't know how I did it, but I remember being so nervous getting up in front of the sixty people that were there that day that I was shaking. My heart was pounding. But I did it! And I got a standing ovation! People seemed to like my songs, and they asked me to write and perform more of them! Little by little, the fear diminished, and I now can get up and sing with confidence, and I can actually enjoy the experience. The fear was replaced with excitement. The physical "symptoms" of feeling that fear were the same as the ones I felt with excitement! I had a change in my perspective. Butterflies were a good thing!! Who knew?

I didn't get over this fear easily or quickly, but I pushed myself, and for the last ten years or so, I have been writing and singing spiritual songs, songs for grievers, and songs for soldiers. It seems that my lyrics move people, and my voice doesn't need to sound like Celine Dion's!!

ANGER

A strong feeling of annoyance, displeasure, or hostility.

Can you recall an instance when someone or something made you so angry that you couldn't think of anything else? Maybe you thought you were treated unfairly, betrayed, or blamed for something you didn't do. Rarely do we experience fear and anger while feeling happy or loving. Instead, we begin with a loss (or what we perceive as a loss), *then* we feel fear which we have trouble controlling. Remember, when we are out of control, we will grab at anything we think we *can* control.

So, by replacing that fear with anger, we may feel more in control of the fear, but really, we just added another boulder to our cans with the anger. When my daughter died, I was angry. I was angry at God, angry that I lost my only child, angry at the world and the unfairness of it all.

When my husband cheated on me, I first felt that loss … Loss of my life as I knew it, loss of my marriage. I was afraid I would never have the kind of relationship I wanted. Then, I felt angry. Now, I know feeling the loss was bad enough, but I certainly felt completely out of control. At least by substituting anger for the loss and fear, I felt like I had some control. But did I? I don't think so. I gave myself to the anger. That created yet another boulder. Do you think I had any positive thoughts or feelings during these times? NO! Not one. And I couldn't understand why I couldn't feel anything good. Poor me. Light? What was that? Since I had not yet found IN-lightenment, I basically just held on to that anger and used it for fuel. I'm sure you know where I'm going with this. It was unhealthy. The opposite of someone in the light is someone in the dark, and in the dark is where these negative emotions hold you and keep you. Now that I practice the theories I have put forward in this book, if this happened to me today, I certainly would handle the situation differently! It doesn't mean I would not feel the hurt or anger, but I would now recognize it as a potential spiritual oil spill, and I could stop it with meditation, acceptance, and letting go … just a few of the lessons we will be learning, beginning with Chapter 5. That is the purpose of this book. In my early stages of uncovering some of these principles, not only did I not know what I needed was to be in the light, but even if I had known, I had no idea how to find it. I was stuck in the mud. Can you think of an instance in your life that began with a loss (or perceived loss) that made you angry? Could you have any good feelings with that? One more boulder for your growing pile. And on top of that pile that is growing, along comes resentment, blame, revenge, and more.

RESENTMENT

Bitter indignation at having been treated unfairly.

First, I felt the loss, then anger, followed by a big helping of resentment. Not only do we get another boulder, but we create more losses—loss of trust, hope, relationships, and faith. Resentment combines so well with fear, anger, and disappointment. I get heavy inside just thinking about this! If we feel mistreated or wronged by another person, we could lose that person (by choice or circumstance), but we can't seem to lose the feeling of resentment.

I lost a child. My only child. That loss created a fear in me ~ fear that I would never recover or ever smile again. Fear that no one would be there for me in my old age. Those fears pointed me to anger, followed by resentment. How unfair it all seemed. Not everyone has lost a child, but everyone has felt the great loss of a loved one, a relationship, a job, or something that was important to them. Sometimes as we look back, we see that in many instances, we even felt those feelings for small things, which we made into bigger things with our negative thoughts.

Acceptance is never the first emotion we feel. But acceptance doesn't load another boulder into our buckets, and yet, for some reason, it's the negative feelings that always come first. I think it's because those feelings are the ones we have used for so long, they are just our "go-to." Then we get fixated on the negative emotion we are living at the moment. We want to tell everyone about what we are feeling, and we wear it like a cheap suit. Ego loves this indignant reaction to feeling mistreated or wronged. It loves to go down the road, stopping at every negative emotion, including judgment, hate, and revenge.

Now, let's say you feel responsible in some way (real or perceived) for your loss. Instead of landing on resentment, you might focus on regret. Great. That one will not only get you a boulder, but a lot of self-doubt, pity, guilt, and despair, which (you guessed it) brings even more spills and boulders.

BLAME

To assign responsibility for a fault or wrong.

Blame seems to go with resentment. We have to blame someone or something for our unhappiness. We blame God, our boss, our spouse or partner, our children, the dog, the weather, the traffic, or anything else we can find. We're angry about the situation; we have resentment, and if we can blame someone or something else, then we think we'll feel better. Nope! Has that ever worked for you? It just loads you down more. Ego loves blame!

Before I became IN-lightened, I blamed God for taking my child away. I was swirling in negative emotions, and light was nowhere to be found. I needed another perspective. I now know and understand what a huge oil spill this creates. Today, I let the blame go with the knowledge that it's no one's fault. Things just happen, especially bad things. I accept that, although it's not always easy to do. I don't always like what happens, but acceptance is not the same as liking it. It's just accepting it as it is with the realization that blame only intensifies the negativity.

For most of us, before becoming IN-lightened, when we blame, we think about it, dwell on it, and it takes us further away from the light, which we can't even entertain as a possibility when we're in the middle of "boulder building!" We might think that blaming someone or something else takes the heat off us, but it does not. Instead, it makes a boulder that adds to the unbearable weight we are already carrying around. Sometimes I think it's pretty amazing just how many boulders we can hold without imploding.

REVENGE

The action of inflicting hurt or harm on someone for an injury or wrong suffered at their hands.

After running through the maze of negativity filled with anger, resentment, and blame, our minds want to conjure up all kinds of revenge scenarios. Have you ever thought about getting revenge? It probably felt good at first, maybe even justified. Perhaps someone cut you off in traffic, and your first thought was to flip them off or yell at them (even though they couldn't hear you!) or maybe even return the favor and cut them off, which could result in an accident. You and your ego are reacting here, and this is never a good or healthy thing for you. Prepare for a big spill to come your way.

I remember a case in San Diego of a woman who was married to a prominent lawyer. He found a younger woman and left his wife with their four children. I followed that case and recently watched the movie about it. As I saw her spiral down after the loss of her marriage, it was easy to see how all that anger for her husband and the current situation could cause her to behave in a really bizarre way. She blamed her misfortune on her husband and his new wife.

As her anger and resentment built, she told everyone about it. She let it take over her life, then plotted and planned one revenge after another until she finally ended up killing both her husband and his new wife while they were sleeping. As a result, she will spend the rest of her life in prison. This is pretty extreme, but many people going through bad times do think of these kinds of revenge scenarios, even if they don't follow through on them.

So much negativity; so many boulders.

SHAME/GUILT

Shame is a feeling of guilt, an emotion typically associated with a negative evaluation of the self.

Shame is another rough emotion for us to live with. It creates feelings of distress, exposure, mistrust, powerlessness, and worthlessness. Nothing good in any of those!

I once knew a nice man who carried a secret with him. He also had a lot of shame about it. This secret was about something he did as a teenager. At the time, he wasn't equipped to deal with it. He couldn't tell his parents, or anyone, for that matter. He had too much shame and guilt. He didn't want anyone to know about it. Somewhere along the way, he decided or read something that told him he should be ashamed of himself. It affected his feelings about who and what he was. He was afraid that someone would find out. He kept his secret to himself and buried it with the boulders he created because of it. He stopped feeling good about himself and developed a load of insecurities that caused other unwanted behaviors.

Of course, we can feel shame and guilt if we feel responsible for something that happens in our lives. Maybe we hurt someone. How long must we carry it around? And how can we move past this horrible emotion? We will explore all of these negative feelings again, along with how to ease them, as we cleanse our spiritual oil spills a little later in Chapter 5 when we discuss Spiritual Cleansing. But first, believe it or not, there are more spiritual oil spills to mention ...

JEALOUSY/ENVY

Envy is wanting what someone else has. Jealousy is worrying that someone will take what you have.

It's no fun to feel envy or jealousy because both make you feel inadequate. Does that surprise you? If you've had a life of self-doubt, insecurity, and inferiority (as a result of your losses), then it's no wonder that other negative emotions will have a lovely breeding ground in your soul.

You might even have a decent life, but if your neighbor puts a fantastic pool in her yard, you may very well envy that. And then, if she invites your boyfriend over for a swim, on top of the envy, you will feel jealousy. We have all felt these feelings. But isn't jealousy fear-based? You are afraid you will lose something if you worry it will be taken away.

Again, it begins with loss (or perceived loss). And if you're having feelings of not being good enough, then jealousy and envy are easy to feel. I envied songwriters for years as I watched them sing their songs at open mike nights. But, instead of motivating me to get up there as well, it did the exact opposite in feeding my insecurities. The more boulders we have in our cans, the more easily these negative emotions can creep in. We know we don't feel as good as we want to, but it's what becomes comfortable and predictable for us and, over time, becomes easier and easier to be our first line of defense. But it's a defense that can never result in a victory.

JUDGMENT

A judgmental person forms lots of opinions, usually harsh or critical ones.

It's interesting that most judgmental people are not open-minded or easygoing. They are probably carrying around lots of boulders and have lots of negative opinions that came from parents, teachers, and other prominent adults in their lives. They are basically unhappy with themselves. One way to elevate our egos is to look down on others. Do you think that when we are being judgmental, we feel good? I don't think so. I think we are unhappy and can only see the downside of everything.

A "judging" person will make a decision after much thought (listening to all the evidence). But a judgmental person just sees it one way. Their way, and that is usually negatively. They have their own ranking system for what's good and what's bad. They can be judgmental about everything ... from another's religious views, race, sexual orientation; even another's clothing. And it follows with ease for a very judgmental person to become hateful. As their harsh opinions spew out, they feel angry inside about what they judge as "bad" or "wrong," and hate can result. Hatred is often associated with intense feelings of anger and disgust ... and perhaps a dose of fear that the thing we are being judgmental about is something we also are afraid of. This judgmental road leads back to even more fear and anger! And the ego loves feeling so right and so righteous. Meanwhile, your soul is being pushed further down as you create even more boulders.

DEFENSIVENESS

An attempt to protect oneself from feeling uncomfortable and from having to view themselves as a failure or otherwise in a negative light.

This spiritual oil spill also has many other negative emotions that can go with it. Let's say someone calls you on something you did. Maybe it's nothing even that big ... like breaking a dish. And maybe it was someone's favorite dish, so you just put it in the trash and hope it's not noticed. This could bring on the fear that you might get caught. And if you do get caught, you would have to face it. Maybe this brings on more fear of losing a relationship over it. Perhaps you are also afraid of being confronted or having to face something you have done. You could just admit to it, but instead, you choose to get angry and defend yourself.

This can also include some resentment on being called out, along with the desire to seek revenge. By this point, you're so deep in it, you can't back down. Another thing to consider here is that being defensive is a way to get the attention off of yourself. And it gives you the opportunity to feel angry and self-righteous, which are not positive feelings but may seem more positive than feeling the guilt or shame that can easily come with a failure being pointed out.

Can you see how this all works together now? One negative feeling on top of another leads to one more boulder on top of our piles.

WORRY/ANXIETY

Worry is a state of anxiety and uncertainty over actual or potential problems.

What may begin as a worry can quickly turn into anxiety. This could be over any real or perceived potential problem. We think about something that could happen and show physical symptoms as though it really has happened. Our heart rate and blood pressure become elevated. We can't eat or sleep. We can become fixated on this worry as it moves to full-on anxiety.

Believe me; there is no light when you are in a state of worry or anxiety. And it has been my personal experience, as well as my witnessing of others' experiences, that when worry is dominating our thoughts, we often bring what we are worried about to fruition. So then, it might be safe to say that worry actually begins in a fear state too. After my husband cheated on me, I believed and was afraid that it would happen again. I wasn't able to completely trust or be 100 percent committed to another relationship. I was dragging that boulder with me, and it was heavy. So heavy. I certainly wasn't staying present; instead, I was dwelling on the past and worrying about my future.

What I have learned is that when we are afraid of something that *could* happen, it's easy to move into a deeper fear that it *will* happen. It clouds our judgment and creates behaviors that feed into our worry. We feel out of control. This can result in anger, resentment, blame, and all those other debilitating emotions we have been talking about. Just how many boulders can we hold? As we live in this anxiety state, filled with fear, acting in ways that feed more into our fears, we are moving head-on to some of the heaviest and biggest boulders of all ... disconnection, despair, and hopelessness.

DISCONNECTION

Disconnection is the state of being isolated or detached.

Have you ever had a situation that has consumed you, your thoughts, and everything you do? The result is that you don't want to or are unable to connect with another person. You don't want to go out, talk, or get help. You feel helpless and frozen. You don't think there is another person in this world who could relate to what you are feeling or understand where you are in your life at this moment. This was exactly how I felt when I lost my daughter. I felt like someone was standing on my chest. I could barely breathe. Nothing anyone could say was going to make me feel better. No one could possibly understand my grief. I had disconnected from the world, which at the time, I believed no longer had anything in common with me, nor I with it.

Feeling good and anything associated with feeling good was not in my repertoire of feelings. I had already run the gamut of every spiritual oil spill we have mentioned until I landed on disconnection.

I felt isolated and alone ... as I was heading for despair.

DESPAIR/HOPELESSNESS

Despair is the complete loss or absence of hope.

Hopelessness is a very intense feeling. It can come with misery, desperation, discouragement, anguish, agony, and distress. People in despair may get up every day and go about their business, but there is no joy in life. It can mark the end of the road for many and cause thoughts of suicide or the actual act of suicide. When I was participating in a grief group, I noticed that many of the grieving parents in my group had lost their children to suicide. Sometimes they didn't even know that their child was depressed. They were going through the motions of life, but inside they felt hopeless. They had one boulder too many. They had more spiritual oil spills than they could handle, and their boulders were just too heavy to carry any further. There seemed to be no relief from this degree of heaviness.

It can happen at any age. We have all had moments of feeling helpless and without hope. We feel out of control, and we can't see a way out or, more importantly, a way *into* the light. We can barely acknowledge that such a thing as light exists. We feel alone and hopeless.

Believe it or not, there are a lot more of these negative feelings, but I have chosen the most common ones that we are all familiar with. How can we find our way out of these feelings that weigh us down? Have you ever gone to an arcade? One of the more common games is called "Whack-a-Mole" or something similar, which is a table with a bunch of holes. Inside each hole is a puppet. All the puppets are sticking up out of the holes. You have a big rubber hammer, and you are trying to hammer all the puppets down, but they just keep popping back up. You try and try to hammer them all down, but they just won't stay down.

Think of each one of those puppets as one of our spiritual oil spills. How can we keep away from all those negative feelings so that we stop having these spills? To see our way clearly to spiritual cleansing and becoming IN-lightened, we must first acknowledge that there are certain spiritual truths within which the Universe operates. And since we are all the same, these apply to everyone.

CHAPTER 4

Ten Spiritual Truths

In Chapter 1, many "what if's" were presented. I'd like to take that a step further and adopt some of those ideas as spiritual truths. Once we have accepted that the Universe is indeed working for us and with us, it's much easier to spiritually cleanse our many oil spills because we will know where we came from and where we should be heading. It's okay to look at the past as we try to understand where we've been and how we got here, but knowing where we are heading gives us the direction we need to stay on the path.

It's sort of like going to a new place in a part of the world we have never seen before. We've heard about it, but we just can't imagine what it might be like. It's a lot easier to get there with a roadmap. First, we would familiarize ourselves with the layout, look for hazards, and find points of interest along the way. Think of this spiritual journey with enthusiasm, wonder, and excitement.

If you've been collecting boulders for many years and have had many spiritual oil spills with many negative emotions, then this might take some work! We must look at this a different way than how we have been looking at it up until now. And like anything new we take on, there is a learning curve. There is a reason that they talk about having a "spiritual practice." This is not something you do once and then it's over. Unclogging your trash can will take some doing, but once you get a glimpse of the light, feel the weights coming off you, and see evidence of these spiritual truths in your own life, then the real spiritual cleansing can begin.

Again, Spirituality is not religion. It's available to everyone, no matter what your religion may be. Spirituality is a connection to the light, God, the Universe, Spirit, Source, or whatever name you wish to give it. I use them interchangeably because they all mean the same thing to me! Spirituality is connecting with the light and also to each other. It's an uncovering of the pure soul you were born to be and a journey back to your real self. Since we all begin with a clean soul, then we are all born with spiritual truths, and deep inside, we all know them to be true. Hopefully, as you read them, you will be reminded of what you already hold deep inside.

SPIRITUAL TRUTH #1

We are all the same inside.

We are all born clean, pure, sweet souls. We are naturally spiritual. We *are* Spirit! We don't have to learn Spirituality; we are born of it! We are souls having a human journey. What makes us different is the different experiences we have and how we handle them. We learn to take on opinions, judgments, and biases from those we meet along the way. We learn all the fear and negative behavior patterns as we are trying to cope with our lives, disappointments, and losses. We are really all on the same journey, not trying to find something new but, rather, finding our way back to what is already there and has always been there. It never leaves us, but, rather, we leave it as we cover it up with what becomes our "coating."

Cocoon was a movie about some beings who came to earth from another planet. They all had different outer coatings to look like earthlings so that they could communicate with us here. However, when they were alone, they would step out of those coverings to expose a lighted being with a very bright aura surrounding them. Every one of those beings looked exactly the same in that form. They were all connected to the Source ... the light. The same is true for all of us humans. We, too, are pure Spirit and light. We just lose touch with it along the way.

Let's accept as a spiritual truth that we are all the same inside our souls, and we are all connected to the same source. We must rid ourselves of the boulders we have been carrying around so that we can get back to what we are and always have been—pure Spirit.

SPIRITUAL TRUTH #2

Everything happens for our highest good, even when we can't see it.

"Oh really," you are saying. What could possibly be good about cancer, losing a child, or being in a crippling automobile accident? Well, the actual event, of course, isn't good. Yes, those traumatic events are game changers, but good can and does come out of them in some form. It may be a game-changer, but it doesn't have to be game over.

How many times have you heard of someone going through cancer treatment saying that it has been the best thing that ever happened to them? They feel like they now have an opportunity to reevaluate their lives. They see what is most important and value that every day. They see each relationship in a new and deeper way. They discover the joy of having gratitude, something we just can't see or feel when we are in the midst of all the spiritual oil spills.

Believe me, I ran the gamut of negative feelings when my daughter died. I had no happy moments, no gratitude for anything, and I didn't think I could go on. I couldn't listen to the music I had always loved so much. I had nothing to smile about, and truthfully, I don't think I wanted to feel better. Then a friend of mine, who was also a psychologist, gave me a different perspective. He said that when you feel like a door has just slammed shut in your life, you can look at it one of two ways:

1. The first way is to see the door slamming right in front of you, and you have nowhere to go. Your life and everything good is behind you. OR…

2. You can see it as the door closing *behind* you, and everything and anything possible lies ahead of you.

There are unlimited experiences beyond that doorway. It's an interesting perspective, and it did make sense to me intellectually, but emotionally, I still felt horrible. Then over time, I began to see opportunities to go on, feel gratitude, and honor my daughter. Now, I couldn't do much for the first few years, but after a while, I started to write songs about it. My daughter always encouraged me with my music, and one day it just sort of happened. An idea popped into my head, and I couldn't *not* write it. I call that divine intervention! It just flowed out of me. The thought that my writing would have made Holland happy, made me happy.

I sent that song to a national grief group that was having their yearly conference. I thought maybe they might have a use for it. The executive director called me and asked me to come sing it. Once again, I tried not to do that, but he wouldn't let me off the hook. He said, "You will be singing to a room full of people who feel the same way as you do. It will help them, and it will change your life." I had already performed at the spiritual center, but this would be in front of a thousand people. Was I nervous? You bet. But I did it and found that my songs gave comfort to other bereaved parents.

Since then, I have also created and presented a workshop called "When the Music Stops" about how we can once again have music and joy in our lives after such a huge loss. I started to feel like I had a life with some purpose in it. That's a good thing! None of this would have happened without the devastating loss of my child. So, the worst cloud in the world for me had a silver lining. The Universe gave me a gift and a reason to go on. And I got to experience the joy of helping others.

SPIRITUAL TRUTH #3

There is only one presence and one power.

It's the same presence and power for all of us: one and only one. We share in it equally, and it is always there for us. If you turn on a light in a room, then leave that room and close the door, you can no longer see the light. Is it still there? Of course, it is. Like Spirit, it is there even when you can't see it. It's there even when you turn away from it. It's always there and always available to you, me, and everyone. We can walk back into that room again anytime, and the light will still be there. It just *is*. That is the spiritual presence and power I am talking about.

When you are in despair, it is described by some as spiraling down into the darkness. But remember, there is still light even in the darkness, and it's there for us. This one presence and one power is all around us and inside us. All of us. All the time. Every minute of every day. Even Jesus said, "The Father and I are one" (John 10:30). When I hear some of the things Jesus said, I think there's a possibility that he was trying to help us on the path to Spirituality … not religion. After all, there was no such thing as Christianity during the life of Jesus. Christianity came after he died. So, I have always wondered, what exactly was he teaching? Perhaps it was Spirituality for all, regardless of religion.

Religion is manmade. Spirituality has always been, just like the one presence and one power has always been. There is no separation between me, you, and this one presence and one power. And on top of that, this one power and one presence is only good. Just because we may not yet be able to see the good in situations where we believe there is no opportunity for good does not mean good is not present.

It's just like the light in the room with the door closed. Yes, we sometimes don't see it (or don't want to see it), but it's always there. And when things aren't looking good, still there must be good in it!

SPIRITUAL TRUTH #4

When you move with the Universe, it moves with you, through you, and for you.

So, what does it mean to "move with the Universe"? Some call it being "One with the Universe." Both mean being aware of everything around you, being aware of your world … the Universe. If you are not aware, you will miss the many little gifts that happen each day, like how amazing it is to see the sunshine, how great your banana tasted this morning, or how good it feels to find a perfect parking space. And if you notice one thing, then you get to feel "in the flow" for that moment. And for the moment that you get to feel in the flow, you feel happiness and peace because noticing these gifts gives you a chance to be grateful.

When you are making boulders, you are focused on all the negativity that causes spiritual oil spills. You are focused on what you feel bad about, so you look for more negativity and can miss the little gifts that are there for you.

For example, just today, I went out to the grocery store and got a great parking space. I noticed and took a moment to say "thank you" to the Universe. That action made me feel good. Who doesn't like getting a gift? I appreciated it. I felt like I must be "in the flow," and that thought also made me feel good. When I went inside the store, I felt like connecting with another human soul. So, I did. That connection made me smile, and the other soul smiled too. If I was locked in negativity, I wouldn't have talked to anyone. I wouldn't have noticed anything. And I would have stayed stuck in that negativity, surrounded by my load of boulders.

The Universe is trying to give us gifts, and seeing those gifts, no matter how small, will not only keep us in the flow but will give way to the spiritual cleansing we are seeking.

SPIRITUAL TRUTH #5

Everything that happens ... just happens.

I love this truth because it leaves no room to be a victim of life or the Universe. If the Universe brings things that are for your growth and higher good, then everything is a gift. I know that traumas and losses are never what we want. Those are not the gifts. The gift is not what happens but, rather, how you handle what happens. It's what you do with it.

What hangs us up is thinking, "Why did this happen to me?" or "What did I do to deserve this?" I'm here to tell you that there is no answer to "why." The answer is, "because it is." I can ask all day why my daughter died. There is no answer no matter how many times I ask the question. If you have a child born with Cerebral Palsy, you can ask "why" a million times. The answer is "because it is." The answer to all why questions is the same. Because it is.

Everything that happens ... just happens. The Universe didn't do it to us. It just happened. What we do with it, how we handle it, determines how many more boulders we put into our cans or how many we could remove to lighten our souls. If blaming God or the Universe could help, then why doesn't that make us feel any better? If we resent our situation, then why doesn't that make us feel better? Those feelings don't ever make us feel better, and they can't. They just make more spiritual oils spills, and that makes us feel worse. And all those boulders that result keep us out of the flow. We must have faith, give up control, and trust that *everything* is ultimately in our best interest and for our spiritual growth (the reason we are here in the first place!), no matter how horrible it initially seems.

SPIRITUAL TRUTH #6

There is nothing you can't do or be.

I wish I had known this truth when I was a young girl, and I only dreamed about music being a big part of my life. I didn't believe this one, that's for sure. When we have boulders of insecurity and feelings of low self-esteem, we are held back by the *belief* we aren't good enough and the fear that keeps us from trying. These are limiting beliefs, and they are not true!

Where that comes from isn't as important as the belief itself. I had the talent. I had the ability. What I didn't have was the belief that I could do it. It wasn't until I was in my sixties that I began to live my dream. I could have buried myself in the loss of all the years that I didn't act. That would have held me back even further. I could have chosen not to act on the opportunity that came much later in my life as though it was just too late for me. But for some reason, circumstances (the Universe) opened a portal for me to step through. Thank God I did step through it.

When the music director told me she would not sing my songs and that I would have to do it myself, I was hurt and angered and felt that my music was being rejected. I could have stopped there and given up. But when my friend encouraged me, I dug down and went for it. I don't know why or how I did it, but I did. So, it all worked out. I was able to let go of my hurt and take another tack. The Universe knew all along! I chose (unconsciously) to move with the Universe ... and the result was more than I ever thought possible.

If you want it, or think you want it, then you must go for it. Failure is not failure if you try and it doesn't work out. Failure is not trying. Not trying will haunt you way more. And even if you do try and it doesn't work out, you can feel good about trying! And in trying, other doors may open, and other experiences will result. Just another example of moving with the Universe so that it can work with you, through you, and for you.

SPIRITUAL TRUTH #7

Inner peace comes from being ... not doing.

I am here just to *be*. I am not my disease, my misfortunes, my mistakes, or my past. I am not my accomplishments, my career, my money, or my possessions. I am not my thoughts or my emotions ... I just *am*. You just are. You are not the "product" of a dysfunctional family, or the son of an alcoholic father, the daughter of an abusive mother, the victim of a crime, the parent of a dead child, or someone who came from a poor family. The list goes on and on. But these are all just things, and they are not who we really are. We may *have* these things, but we are not these things. Yet, somehow, we feel we are, as though they make up our identity. Our outer coatings differentiate us from others, but that's not who we are either. We are Spirit, just like the characters in *Cocoon*. Uncover us, and we are beautiful, radiant souls—every one of us.

As we make our way through life and circumstances, we find ourselves getting heavier and heavier. We don't feel peace inside. We try to *do* things to find that peace. We seek temporary escapes from this unrest with food, alcohol, drugs, sex, television, and anything that will keep us from feeling the lack of peace. (Isn't this another loss … the loss of peace?) With all we do, we can't seem to find that inner peace, so we stop trying as though it's not there. But just like the light, that inner peace is always there too. It's just covered up with our heaviness, and we get even heavier with the addition of each boulder.

We need to stop doing and start being. We are soul. Perfectly created and fully loaded with all we need. The soul is pure, and none of our worldly things are needed by the soul. Our soul is screaming to get out from under all the boulders we are holding onto. It is begging to become IN-lightened. It wants to just *be*. And it wants to *be* with us. We need to go inside, into the silence, and spend time with our souls.

SPIRITUAL TRUTH #8

Gratitude is the ultimate spiritual practice.

Two definitions of gratitude in the dictionary are:

1. The quality of being thankful; readiness to show appreciation for and to return kindness.
2. An emotion of the heart, excited by a favor or benefit received; a sentiment of kindness or goodwill towards a benefactor; thankfulness.

Think of a time when something happened, and you were truly grateful for it. Maybe it was a Christmas present you had wanted for a long time, an honor bestowed upon you in school or at work, or a kindness that someone showed you. Remember how you felt inside? That warm, loving feeling that made your heart swell. Was there any room left for anger, fear, or resentment? No. Gratitude would be the only feeling that you had. It fills your heart and makes you smile inside. It feeds your soul. When you are feeling gratitude, you can't feel anything negative. It's just not possible.

In gratitude, you don't think of your losses, disappointments, past, or future. You are in the flow of the Universe, and you have inner peace. You feel that wonderful feeling inside, and it warms you all over. We have many, many occasions during each day to feel this way—every day. But we get so caught up in our challenges, problems, and negative feelings that go with them that we don't notice everything we can be grateful for. In fact, when we're in those negative emotions, gratitude is nowhere to be found. What if I told you that gratitude, all by itself, can clean spiritual oil spills and crush boulders? It can. It comes with the love, kindness, and joy that fills and lightens your soul.

SPIRITUAL TRUTH #9

There is no spot where God is not.

I am still using God/Universe/Spirit/Light/Source interchangeably. They are one and the same. We are one with it. It's everywhere. Again, it's all around us and inside us. All the time, even when we're struggling. We might not feel it or notice it, but I promise you, it's there. So, it's safe to say that there is no spot where God is not! Rather than try to explain it, I wrote a song about it! I'd like to share just the chorus with you:

> *There is no spot where God is not,*
> *There is no place that God forgot.*
> *There's just one presence and one power in my life,*
> *I feel the Spirit all around.*
> *I hear the word without a sound,*
> *Divine love flows through me, and it will never stop,*
> *There is no spot where God is not.*

Even in our spiritual trash cans, full of boulders, there are small spaces. That is not just air or dead space. It's God. And with the removal of each boulder, that space will then be filled with more God, and with that comes all the wonderful feelings that being in the flow can and will bring to you.

SPIRITUAL TRUTH #10

We are here to learn and grow spiritually.

Have you ever wondered why we are here? Or what is the purpose of this life? I have, and after many hard knocks, I think we are here to learn and grow spiritually. I never did think I was here just to make it through another day, have fun, or party with my friends. I never got much satisfaction from that. Yes, it's fun, but I always felt there had to be more; I just didn't know what it was.

When we were in school, we were taught to read. That skill helped us in everything we did and do. But no one teaches us how to grow spiritually. We must land on that one ourselves. The Universe gives us many opportunities for this growth. Some of the lessons are very hard. *Very* hard! Have you ever taken Geometry or Calculus? You know what I'm talking about! Still, you had to take that class if you wanted to elevate educationally. By the same token, if you want to elevate spiritually, you must take some hard classes and learn new ways of doing things. And the Universe is more than happy to provide these lessons. They are for your higher good. You can fight it, or you can step into it.

I'm not saying this will be easy. It's not. But it's worth the effort. Open your heart and mind and ask the Universe to bring it on. There are only rewards, and there is no downside. So, there is nothing to lose by trying and everything to gain. Once you have a taste of inner peace and being in the flow, you will want to get there again and be there as often as possible. Are you ready to take the first step towards your IN-lightenment? Let's go!

CHAPTER 5

Spiritual Cleansing

We all have spills, clogs, and boulders. We are spiritually out of alignment. By reacting to every situation with negative emotions, we stay out of alignment unless we find a way to empty our trash cans and cleanse our souls. Remember that we *are* soul. We always have been soul. We have just forgotten how to respond as the souls we were born to be, and the more boulders we have collected, the more out of alignment we become. We still have the ability (and, I believe, the desire) to be free of the boulders that weigh us down. We just need to go back to the beginning.

How many of us took a foreign language in school? I took three years of Spanish. I could read, write, and speak it. But I never really used it. Today, I can only remember a few words, but putting a sentence together with verb conjugation is almost impossible for me now.

Spirituality is the same principle. You must practice it, use it, know it, and feel it until it becomes your go-to and what is most familiar to you. I promise you; it's all there inside you. You will know it when you feel it again! It will feel amazing. It will feel like seeing an old friend or going back home. Clearing the path to Spirituality comes from becoming IN-lightened, and becoming IN-lightened comes from connecting with Spirit, God, Universe, the Light, Source. It comes from nurturing our souls. We need to turn inward rather than look outside ourselves for happiness, joy, and peace.

I want to emphasize that we do not need to be "fixed." We are not broken. We are not "less than." We are perfect and whole, and everything we need to be happy is already inside us. We just need to unload the boulders and fill that remaining space with a different perspective and a different way of reacting to what is happening in our lives. We need to get more familiar with the positive feelings that happen when we are "in the flow." I can tell you that you can't feel negative and positive in the same moment. Here is a list of some of the positive feelings you will be becoming more familiar with during your cleansing:

Acceptance	Forgiveness	Compassion
Gratitude	Confidence	Contentment
Happiness	Tolerance	Empathy
Patience	Faith	Joy
Peace	Hope	Love

Who wouldn't want to feel all these wonderful emotions, right? You can, but you can't feel them along with the negative feelings. Can you imagine feeling resentment towards another person and also feeling compassion or empathy at the same time? Or think about feeling judgmental about an issue and feeling tolerant at the same time. Hardly possible! They are opposites.

Earlier, we identified the negative emotions that cause our spills. Our goal is to move away from those negative emotions to the positive ones. We want to reprogram our thinking and responses to our problems and boulder-building situations. To make this move successfully, there are a few important "spiritual cleansers" to keep in mind.

LETTING GO

Letting go is one of the best spiritual cleansers of all. We all have boulders, but for some reason, once we have them in our trash cans, we just can't seem to get rid of them. That's because we hold on. We hold on to what happened to us, and more importantly, we hold on to the feelings that went with it. It's like being in quicksand, and every boulder makes us heavier as we sink further. Letting go is the rope that can pull us out.

I realize that this is easier said than done! Of course, we don't want to hold on to things that hurt us, but we fall into this ditch, and then the walls of the ditch seem too steep to climb up out of. It takes effort and a lot of courage. It takes acceptance, patience with yourself, faith in the Universe, and faith in yourself.

Notice that acceptance, patience, and faith are nowhere to be found on the spiritual oil spill list. We need to practice replacing those negative feelings that cause the spills with positive feelings. Patience comes into play because, at first, you will still want to go where it's more comfortable, and unfortunately, that is to the negative.

Let me give you an example. I was married to what I would call a "playboy," or at least he thought he was. I caught him cheating on me more than once. The first time was really the end of our marriage, but I stayed a few years more. Why? I was *afraid* of being divorced and alone. I loved our life and friends, and I didn't want to *lose* them, and I had some *less than, not enough* feelings about myself. All negative. So, I stayed and was very unhappy. I talked about it nonstop. It consumed me. I was angry, resentful, and felt like a victim. It affected all aspects of my life. Finally, I had the courage to leave. And still, I carried that with me. I just couldn't accept it. I talked about it, thought about it, wished negative things on my then ex-husband, and took those boulders into my subsequent relationships as I lost trust and vowed never to marry again.

I actually believed that all men cheat. I had not yet been exposed to Spirituality and what it could have done to help me. Never once did I think of having compassion for this person who also had a trash can full of his own boulders of insecurity and whatever else led him to need to keep feeding his sexual ego.

It wasn't until many years after the divorce, as he was dying of cancer, that I was able to talk with him and forgive him. It was like a huge weight was lifted from my shoulders.

I realized that forgiving was actually a gift to myself, and only after that act of forgiveness was I able to finally let go and move on emotionally. I spent years holding on to this one, but now I'm free of it. This is much better! I can tell you from my own experience that acceptance is a hard one to do, but the rewards are great. And the same goes for forgiveness. It may let the forgiven "off the hook," but the real gift is to the forgiver. If you work internally to forgive someone, that's great. But if the opportunity exists to reach out to let that someone know you forgive them, be brave and do so. The reward will be there for you.

Can you think of a situation in your life right now that has you bogged down? Can you allow yourself to accept the situation? You don't have to like it, but liking it is not the same as acceptance. Can you accept it as just one of those things that happens? If you can, without trying to get an answer to why, then you are on your way to letting go. And if you can forgive the other party, you will let go even further. And while you're at it, why not forgive yourself for taking so long?? Once you do, you will remember how it feels to let go, and next time, it won't be so hard.

CHANGE YOUR PERSPECTIVE

There is always more than one perspective in any given situation. Our current perspectives come from all the years and experiences of our life up until this point. Some say that we are souls on a human journey. I ask that you turn that thought around to "we are humans on a soul journey." That small change in perspective sheds a different light on things. Then, just for a minute, try to see the negative feelings as the human perspective, and the positive feelings as the soul perspective.

By replacing our reactions with different perspectives and behaviors, we will be feeding and nurturing our souls with positive feelings more while leaving less and less room for all the negativity we have been storing. As you begin looking at every situation from your soul's perspective, you will make way for more goodness in your everyday experiences and your entire life.

For example, let's say you have a falling out with someone you thought was your friend. Perhaps they pointed out something about yourself to you. Maybe you often interrupt. Maybe they see that you drink too much. Maybe they see you as a permissive person who gets taken advantage of by others. The reason could be anything that makes you (and your ego!) feel less than. Your initial reaction is negative. From your perspective, you might be thinking this person is not a friend. They probably never really liked you, and they wanted to hurt you. You feel betrayed and demeaned. Your emotions run from being defensive to angry and more. You can only think of all the negatives that might have caused this friend to speak to you like that. You can't imagine there is anything good to feel about this person. That's *your* perspective.

But your friend's perspective might be completely different. They love you. They are worried about you and only said something because, from *their* perspective, they thought telling you might let you see something different and, as a result, help you in some way, but you can't even think of looking at it from a different perspective through your anger. Brace yourself because more boulders are rolling your way.

What if you had some gratitude that you had a friend who cared enough to tell you the truth? What if you had an appreciation of the gift of that knowledge? Think of what you could do with that knowledge. Think of all the possibilities of how that knowledge might improve your life. Then emotionally think of how you would feel inside in the first scenario and how differently you would feel inside in the second scenario. It would be quite different. Are you beginning to see how a perspective change and a positive spiritual feeling in place of a negative reaction could be worth trying??

EMBRACE YOUR PROBLEMS

I'm sure we can agree that we all have problems from time to time. Every one of us faces challenges and disappointments. No one has a perfect life with everything going exactly as they want all the time.

Some problems are bigger than others, but they all seem big when we are in the middle of them. Being in the midst of negative feelings as we are creating spills and boulders never feels good. Remember, most of these problems begin with a loss (or a perceived loss). That loss could be something that has already happened or the fear of a loss that will result from the problem. Once we become fixated on that problem and the loss, we get buried under the negative feelings. How can we get out from under those feelings?

What if every problem is a blessing? I know that while we're deep in it, we can't see that as a possibility, but again, how about taking a new perspective? Just for a moment, let's assume that every problem *is* a blessing. Then we need to feel grateful for that blessing and rejoice in the forthcoming lesson. There is always something to learn from every situation, as well as an opportunity for you to have some soul growth. After all, we are here for a soul journey, aren't we?

Look back on your own life to a time when you didn't think you could get through whatever was happening, and you did! Now in retrospect, you even see that what happened was for the best. Maybe you lost your job, and then a better one came along, or you lost a lover, and then you met someone way more wonderful. If someone had told you that way back then, you would not have been able to see it. When you're stuck in the mud, you can't see the future. You can't feel hopeful that anything good is on the way. But now that you are looking back, you do see that it was in your best interest and the best thing that could have happened.

In school, if you are given a difficult math problem to solve, you take on that challenge. If you don't solve it one way, you will try another way. You don't keep trying to solve that problem exactly the same way because you know you can't. You realize your first solution didn't solve the problem. So, trying that same solution, no matter how many times you try it, still won't solve it. You just know you need to try something else. Why not look at this soul journey in a similar way? We get a problem, yet we want to try to solve it the same way, over and over, and it's not working! If anger could fix it, you wouldn't keep ending up with the same negative result. Instead of anger, choose from the list of positive feelings. Try compassion, understanding, tolerance, love.

I know someone who tried to take his own life. Several people close to him had recently died of cancer. There was nothing he could do to help or change that. Those were losses to him. He had many failed relationships and was alone—more loss. During the same time, the economy was in a bad period, and his successful business fell apart. He lost most of his money and felt that he could no longer cope with it or fix it, and he couldn't accept it. He couldn't see a way out. So, he took a bunch of pills, drank a load of alcohol, and sat in his chair waiting to get the hell out. This is despair at its highest (or, I should say, at its lowest!).

Well, the Universe had other plans for him. He slept for two days and was found when he missed an important meeting, and someone came to his house to check on him. He was surprised that he lived through it. He went to counseling and, fortunately, was able to go on. He learned that he had to accept what had happened. Once he accepted it, things started to change for him. He found new and satisfying work, a new and wonderful relationship, new ways of looking at things, and new ways of *feeling* things.

Instead of anger, resentment, despair, and hopelessness, he learned acceptance, compassion, forgiveness, and how to feel good. Something horrible gave way to something good. This ordeal got his attention, and it did turn out to be a blessing, indeed.

If we see everything as a problem, humanly, we will suffer as we see and feel the negatives.

If we see everything as a blessing and respond with our positive soul feelings, we will soar!

The path to Spirituality is not smooth. It's bumpy. It has twists and turns. These bumps are the challenges we all face. If we can see these challenges as blessings, then we will embrace them because we will know that they are gifts, and we will have the faith that even if we can't see it right now, the blessing is on the way! And the bigger the challenges, the greater the gifts. We don't have to focus on the problem. What we need to focus on is our reactions to the problem.

Little things come up each day, all day, that we can practice on. The Universe is trying to help us grow and practice. Today, try being aware of these opportunities. If you spill your coffee, can't find something you are looking for, or are cut off on the freeway, you have opportunities to react differently than with anger, frustration, or blame. Stop for a minute and notice. Then choose another response. The positive ones feel so much better. And many times, I find that a little good humor goes a long way too!

Right now, I'm sitting at my desk, writing this book. I get stuck and don't know just how to say what I'm trying to say sometimes. I have options on how to react. I can feel frustrated and angry. I can even pick up my laptop and throw it against the wall. I can blame my dog for interrupting me. I can start judging my work and feel like I'm a bad writer and I'm just wasting my time. You know what I'm saying here!

Or, I can just go outside for a while and go for a walk, breathe the fresh air, notice some nature, and *know* that the right and perfect words will come. I can choose faith, confidence, and patience. Then I can let go of those negative feelings, change my perspective on things, forgive, and enjoy the problem, which in this example, was obviously a blessing because I needed to take a break anyway. I feel better already! Give it a try. The Universe is calling you!

ALIGN WITH THE UNIVERSE

Let's go back to Spiritual Truth #4: *When you move with the Universe, it moves with you, through you, and for you.* We must know this to be true. That's called faith. All is in divine order and as it should be. We need to step into it and work with it. You have all seen and walked on those moving sidewalks at the airport.

It's moving continuously, and we just have to step on it to move with it. If we don't step on, it will keep moving anyway. We just won't be moving with it. We will either be stuck right there, or we will have to walk on our own next to it without any assistance.

Try thinking of the Universe like that moving sidewalk. It's always moving, always blessing, always there every minute of every day. It doesn't take a day off, close for lunch, slow down, or turn away. It is a pure representation of the positive feelings our soul needs to soar. And those feelings are always available to us ... even through the problems. Especially through the problems.

The Universe represents love and all that goes with it and gladly offers us those same feelings. Those feelings are continuously flowing, and we can tap in at any time. That's why it's called "being in the flow."

By the same token, the Universe has no negative feelings. There are no negative feelings that feed the soul. Not one. The Universe doesn't do anything *to* us. It doesn't put problems in our lives or in our way. Those problems that we all experience are the things that just happen (as in Spiritual Truth #5). The nudges from the Universe come as a gift *after* what happens just happens. It doesn't try to get your attention by giving you the problem. It tries to get your attention by offering you the solution!

The Universe does not get angry at you. It does not resent you if you don't react in a positive way. It doesn't get even. It doesn't punish you by making a problem for you, causing an accident, or taking away one of your loved ones. Those problems are your experiences. They just happen. You can step out of the flow and walk alongside the Universe and try to handle a problem on your own with every negative feeling you are used to, or you can step into the flow and receive every positive feeling the Universe is always offering. There is no limit, and you don't have to *do* anything special to receive it. You just have to align with the Universe. It'll always be yours.

Have faith in it. Trust it. Welcome it. Ask for it. Expect it. Be grateful for it. Once you see for yourself how changing your reaction puts you in the flow, you will want to be there as much as possible.

OPEN UP

You might be saying that you don't know where to start. To that, I would say, "Open up." Try it. You have nothing to lose, but you can and will feel better, happier, and more peaceful. Open your heart. Open your thoughts. Open up to new ideas about dealing with things. Open up to all the wonderful positive emotions that are all around you. Open up to the Universe. It's always open to you. And the more you open up to it, the more it will fill you.

The best way to get started is to trust. Trust that the Universe is there and accessible and working for you. Trust that the Universe knows what it's doing. Even if you think you want something and the Universe doesn't bring it, trust that everything is happening for your best interests and highest good. You might want to let go of some of your desires (or perceived desires) and trust that the Universe knows better. Trust. Trust. Trust. And don't forget to trust yourself and your process. Trust that you are making the right steps to becoming IN-lightened, and soon you will be clearing out your boulders and happily making your way on the path to Spirituality. You will never want to turn back!

Trust that you can have a relationship with the Universe. And, as in any relationship, you need to participate. For example, if you met someone and you thought you'd like to get closer, you would think about them, call them, and want to spend as much time as possible with them. You would want to show them how you feel and how much they mean to you. Think of a relationship with the Universe as the ultimate relationship. Trust it, because it is!

As you open up more, you will begin to see the amazing gifts. Ask for guidance, then open yourself and trust that you will be guided and directed to what's best. Let go of your old feelings and preconceived notions of what's right for you and how things should and shouldn't be. See yourself as a clean slate as you feel the excitement of this amazing journey and what every new day can and will bring.

With some practice, you will soon feel the difference. And what a difference it will be! Accept who you are at this moment and where you are right now. See yourself, and everything you have, as enough. The Universe will respond by giving you even more.

Remember, the Universe does not deal in negatives. It doesn't understand or respond to that kind of energy. But it will respond abundantly to positive thoughts and positive energy. As you are letting go, forgiving, changing perspective, embracing your problems, aligning with the Universe, and opening up, there is one very important element that needs to be a part of it all. This element deserves its own chapter; it's that important. It's called gratitude.

CHAPTER 6

Gratitude

*L*et's begin by trying to define gratitude. I found two interesting definitions in the dictionary:

1. The quality of being thankful; readiness to show appreciation for and return kindness.
2. An emotion of the heart, excited by a favor or benefit received; a sentiment of kindness or goodwill towards a benefactor; thankfulness.

Both of these definitions are a good start, but gratitude is really so much more. These definitions are from the mind, in my opinion. Gratitude, however, is really a feeling in the heart, as in definition #2. It's acknowledging and appreciating how much we have and not taking it for granted. It's a beautiful, heartwarming feeling.

Yes, it's being thankful for something, but it's more than that. We can logically know to thank someone for something they have done because it's the "right thing to do." That's having manners. But to really *feel* gratitude is an overwhelming delicious feeling in the heart. There is no negative thought that can touch gratitude, and when you're in a state of gratitude, you cannot be touched by negative thoughts. When you are truly in gratitude, you can't feel fear, worry, or other negative feelings. It's not possible!

Feeling grateful is right up there with feeling love. It warms you, surrounds you, and enfolds you. Gratitude enhances your life and brings happiness. It deserves your attention and focus! And when you are putting out the feelings of gratitude to the Universe, you will be expressing and acknowledging the abundance in your life. To that, the Universe will respond with even more abundance. That's just the way it works!

On the flip side, if you don't have gratitude and you're always thinking and dwelling on what you don't have, then that's what the Universe "hears," and you will keep getting more of that. It's the Law of Attraction. What you think, you attract. Wayne Dyer said, "Change your thoughts, change your life." If we think we are lacking in our lives, we can't feel gratitude because we don't think we have anything to be grateful for. If we can't feel gratitude, we won't know the beauty of an overflowing heart. At this moment, I am so grateful to have come so far on my road to becoming IN-lightened. Please take a moment right now and think of one thing for which *you* are truly grateful. Maybe it's a person in your life, or an object like a new car, or a favor someone did for you. You feel your heart swell, and you smile. What if you could feel that way most of each day?

I promise you; you do have enough things to be grateful for to fill every day if you are open and awake. Stay aware and take the time to notice. Start by noticing yourself and all that your amazing body does for you. Notice what others do for you. Notice the many gifts you have. Notice what the Universe sends you. Let me help you with a few gratitude exercises that can and will help you discover and feel it.

GRATITUDE EXERCISE #1
~ THE LIST

I highly recommend that you make a list of things you can be grateful for right now, today. Below is my gratitude list. I'm sure you can identify with many things on my list, so feel free to use some of them on your list too! Dwell on those things that resonate with you, not the few that don't apply to you! Feel free to add and subtract items from this list, so it's more personal to you, or just start with a blank piece of paper and make your own list! These are 20 things that come to mind in my life, but there are so many more. And my list is in no particular order. See how many you can claim as your own and how many more you can think of. This list should consist of all the things you have in your life right at this moment.

Having eyes to see everyone and everything around me
The ability to hear music
The ability to taste something wonderful
My health
Shelter
A warm jacket on a cold day
The ability to learn and grow
The joy of smelling something delicious cooking in
    the kitchen
The ability to read, write, and understand
The wonder of nature and how it works
The joy in being able to speak my truth
My dog, cat, or other loving creature
A warm sunny day
Food in my refrigerator to nurture me
A good movie that touches me
Legs and arms that move and respond
A special relationship
The joy of having been a mother
My grandchildren
Being able to feel a great hug

As you make your list, stop for just a moment to reflect on each one. Let's take the first one and appreciate that we have eyes to see. Think of all the things we use our eyes for every day, many times a day. We read the paper or watch the news. We see that spot on our shirt. We play a game on our phone. We watch our child or pet. The list is endless. Can you even imagine life without your eyes? Close them for a few minutes, and you will no longer see these words. Keep your eyes closed and get up and try to walk around. Say thank you to your eyes. What a gift they are.

We have so many gifts that we just get used to them being there in our lives. We take them for granted. But the feeling of knowing gratitude is so amazing that once you feel it, you will start looking for things to be grateful for so you can feel it again. Take each thing on your list, one at a time, and do the same thing you did in thinking of your eyes. Wow! Aren't we amazing? Don't we have so much to be grateful for?

Even during trauma or a difficult time, there are things to be grateful for. When my daughter died, of course, I couldn't see anything good or happy. All I could focus on was my huge loss and the fact that my life would never be the same. I certainly wasn't thinking about the gift of my eyesight, but it was still there, wasn't it? So many of the gifts were still there, but did I notice? Nope. I had to try to change my thoughts and find happiness and gratitude in the fact that at least I had Holland for the time I had her. I had to dig down deep to allow myself to feel any gratitude.

Feeling good was very hard to do. But a friend of mine reminded me that I still had some blessings. She had lived. She was my child. I was her mother. And on top of those blessings, she left behind two amazing babies (they were only 1 and 2 years old when she died). So, I had and have two wonderful grandchildren. Talk about having something to be grateful for! Thank you, God! That realization helped me so much and allowed my heart to feel happy again.

It started slowly and infrequently, but I'm here to tell you that there is nothing better than gratitude to get rid of those boulders. It's like holding up a cross to Dracula!! So, the next time you are having a negative moment, stop. Think instead of something to be grateful for, and you will feel a wonderful shift in the way you feel.

GRATITUDE EXERCISE #2
~ A DAY OF GRATITUDE

I would like you to commit one entire day to this exercise. Pick any normal day so that you can observe all that is regularly there, that, perhaps, you don't normally stop and notice. As you go through your day, I would like you to notice specific things for which you can be grateful. Try to shoot for ten things, but don't stress if you only notice five things the first time. It will get easier, and it's fun to start noticing things from the gratitude state! You are not looking for the same general things as those you wrote on your list in the first exercise. These are things that might happen every day, but on this day, you really stop and notice them as things you are or can be grateful for.

For example, on my list in the first exercise, I mention the ability to taste something wonderful. That's pretty general. However, on my gratitude day, the first thing I noticed was how wonderful my coffee tasted, which is more specific. It always tastes good, but today I had conscious gratitude for it as I noticed it, acknowledged it, and gave thanks for it. Most of us are not in the habit (yet!) of choosing gratitude as a spiritual practice. Please remember that gratitude is the *ultimate spiritual practice*. This is an exercise to get you more used to it. Once you notice something, stop whatever you are doing for just a moment so you can enjoy it and feel grateful for it. You don't want to rush through this. You don't want to just fill your list in 15 minutes so that you can get this over with.

Discover each thing on your way throughout your day. You want the full experience of *feeling* the gratitude in your heart. It should feel amazing and be a feeling that you want to feel more of. So, take a moment, be grateful, say thank you, breathe it in, and just let yourself feel your heart. Choose something you are *really* grateful for, not something you *think* you should be grateful for. Think of something simple … something that you do every day, but today it will feel more special than ever before.

I created this exercise when I was first thinking of ways I could bring more gratitude into my own life. I was surprised at first at just how many things I found! Many were things that I didn't give much special thought to before this day. As a result, I saw these things differently, with more reverence and gratitude. I love the way it feels, and I try to incorporate this into every day. If I can find just one more thing that I hadn't noticed before, I'm so happy … and, of course, grateful!

My Gratitude Day

1. My first sip of coffee. I always enjoy my first sip of coffee, but today, I held on to it. I swirled it in my mouth and felt the warmth and the flavor as I heard myself say, "Mmmm," deeply grateful for this experience. Grateful for being able to taste it. Grateful that coffee was discovered as a beverage!

2. I received an email from a friend I haven't heard from in a while that contained a sweet memory of a trip we took together years ago. That made me smile and feel gratitude for not only the trip we took together, but for her long-term and loyal friendship.

3. The sky is a perfect blue today. Not a cloud to be seen. And the sun is shining. I stepped outside and took a moment to look at each tree and plant within my view as though I had never seen it before. I took my time while being grateful that I *can* see this beauty and stand in awe of awesome nature.

4. I actually noticed and expressed gratitude for the running water in my shower! And it's hot running water! I'm grateful for many modern conveniences, but hot water is the one today!

5. I wrote a letter to my grandchildren with so much gratitude for them in my life that I had tears in my eyes while I was writing.

I told them of my gratitude. My heart is overflowing.

6. I stopped to look at all the pictures hanging on my office wall. I have many, and I looked at each one. I recalled the time they were taken and the memory that goes with each one. I'm grateful for everyone in my family and every sweet memory. I'm so happy (and grateful) that I took the time to stop and look deeply into each photo as love and gratitude filled my heart.

7. I had to run an errand. That gave me a chance to feel grateful for my car. I got in, turned the key, and it just went! I expect it to go without much thought, and I think I have taken that for granted. I really did feel grateful for my car … so I told it!

8. This might sound crazy, but today I noticed toilet paper. What a wonderful invention, and I am grateful for it. Feeling gratitude even for this small thing was wonderful. In fact, all forms of gratitude are wonderful.

9. My desk sits right in front of a window. I love that! If anyone walks by, I see them. There is a lady who walks every day. She waves at me, and I wave back, but I've never met her. Today, I went outside when I saw her. We met, exchanged names, and spoke for a while. I felt gratitude for meeting her, and I'm happy and grateful that I took the time to go outside.

10. I used to have a wonderful Golden Retriever named Joey. He died many years ago. He used to come sit by my desk. Every once in a while, I feel him there. That happened today. I am grateful for that moment, and today I stayed in that moment for several minutes, feeling the gratitude. Amazing!

GRATITUDE EXERCISE #3
~ AWAKEN TO GRATITUDE

Tomorrow morning, please give this exercise a try. Before you get out of bed, take a few minutes to express gratitude for the upcoming day. Thank your heart for beating, your lungs for breathing, your eyes for opening, and anything else in your body that you would like to thank.

Feel and acknowledge gratitude for the special people in your life. Appreciate that you are alive and have the gift of another day. As you express your gratitude, you will realize how many things you have to be thankful for right there before you even put your feet on the floor! That alone will place you in the state of gratitude to start your day. Not to mention that it will just make you happy and joyful.

You can also have gratitude for any negative feeling you had that is now gone or an accident that was avoided. And if something wonderful happened the day before, it's okay to be grateful for it again. Think of the little things that may have happened. By thinking of the little things, you may be surprised how many times a grateful moment is presented to you each day.

As you increase your awareness, you'll be pleasantly surprised at how things show up for you that can put you solidly in the state of gratitude. That feeling will always be a gift, and then you can even have gratitude for the gratitude! I just want to mention that this is not the time for you to think about all you have to do this day, how to deal with any perceived problems you may be dealing with, or how you're going to pay off that nagging bill on your desk. It's *only* time for gratitude. You may have to train your mind at first not to wander off the path, but the feeling you will experience with true gratitude should keep you wanting it more and more.

You can practice this exercise every morning before you begin your day. Can you think of any better way?

GRATITUDE EXERCISE #4
~ KEEPING A GRATITUDE JOURNAL

Some people like to keep a gratitude journal where they can write down what they are grateful for. This is an option for those who like to write or want to record their gratitude journey. You might want to start slowly, just writing a few lines. Or perhaps writing only a few times each week is enough for you. Or you can write every day. It's completely up to you.

Keeping a gratitude journal is not mandatory for your spiritual success, but it seems to be a widely held belief that journaling has many benefits. You can look back and see your progress and how you felt at an earlier time. You can keep a "Spiritual" journal that includes your gratitude work as well as all the feelings you are having at any given time. You can enter a negative feeling you had and how you turned that into gratitude. Just writing it down can make it more real and show you that you are indeed on the right track. It can and will help you become more self-aware as you gain a greater understanding of your feelings.

You can write about what you are grateful for and watch as that list grows. You can look back at an earlier time when you felt big gratitude and feel it again! You will be able to re-visit how you turned a negative into a positive and feel good about each time you did it! You can write your spiritual goals and intentions. Some people swear by it; some don't. You can just give it a try and see how it works for you. It's just an option, not a requirement!

As long as you are feeling and expressing gratitude, you'll be on the right track. But it can be fun to look back at your writings (especially those at the beginning) and see how far you've come. If you have never kept a journal before, this might take some getting used to, but like everything on this spiritual journey, what you practice, you will improve at. If you want to play baseball, you need to practice to get better at it. If you want to learn to play a musical instrument like the piano, only practice will help you master it. The same is true of Spirituality. The more you practice, the better you'll get at it. The more you practice, the more comfortable you will become with it and the more natural it will feel.

Imagine hitting your first home run or playing your first difficult piece at your piano recital. Oh, the joy in those things! Spirituality will also bring you joy as you clear your path to becoming IN-lightened. Like in baseball or the piano, you will never go back to not knowing how to play. Once you are solid on your spiritual path, you will not forget, and you won't ever want to go back to a life without it.

And on days when you may wander a little off the path, you will have all that practice to draw upon, so getting back onto the path will not be that difficult. I had never kept a journal or a diary before, so for me, it took a little getting used to. And I actually felt a little uncomfortable when I began, but it did get easier, until one day, I realized that I couldn't wait for journal time. After that, on many occasions, I was able to work out a feeling as I was writing. And now I'm a writing fool! I say, "Open yourself to a new experience and give it a try!"

GRATITUDE EXERCISE #5
~ PAY IT FORWARD

I love this concept! It's easy to say "thank you" *after* getting what you want. But how about saying "thank you" in advance? For example, say "thank you" for the day that is about to unfold, even when you have no idea what it will bring. Then you can face your day with anticipation and excitement. Say "thank you" to the Universe for guiding and directing you as it brings you each new day. And how about these?

- Thank you for allowing my heart to be fully open to anything and everything.
- Thank you for helping me see and know that everything is for my highest good.
- Thank you for helping me move through my day with grace and gratitude as I let go of all negativities.
- Thank you for giving me the tools to handle any challenges that arise.
- Thank you for the revelations that come with every experience.

Those are just a few examples, but I think you get the picture!

As you pay it forward with these gestures of gratitude, you are also opening up to these things actually happening for you. Why wouldn't you say "thank you" in advance when you have faith that these things will happen as you are aligning with the Universe? Remember how important and powerful your thoughts are.

You can also pay it forward by practicing kindness. See how many smiles you can give away today. It costs nothing, and not only will you make someone else smile, but your own heart will smile too. Open a door for someone else. Talk to a senior citizen. I remember when my mother was in her eighties. She said she felt invisible, as though she wasn't there and felt like she no longer had any value. From that moment on, I prioritized talking to an older person at the grocery store, in any line, or while I was waiting for an appointment. The response was always amazing. They were so grateful that I spoke to them, and I always felt good that I did. Just a little gesture like that to make someone else's day will make yours too. And that gesture will fill you with gratitude and a full heart for having done it.

You can try your own experiment when it comes to paying it forward. The next time you are getting ready to pull into a parking lot, say thank you to the Universe for the perfect parking spot that is going to show up. See it happening in your mind. Then watch how many times you do get a great parking space. You will be surprised!

GRATITUDE EXERCISE #6
~ HOW TO FEEL GRATITUDE IN THE MIDDLE OF A SPIRITUAL OIL SPILL

We already know that you can't feel a negative feeling when you're in the state of gratitude. You can't be grateful and angry at the same time. However, you can call up gratitude when you're having a negative feeling or when you're heading for a big spiritual oil spill. It's a challenge sometimes and not always easy to do, but it can be done. The first thing you must do is develop your own self-awareness. This comes from being present in all that you are doing.

Pay attention to your thoughts and feelings. When you notice that negativity popping up, STOP! Try to identify what you are feeling right at that moment. Breathe. Breathe again! Usually, you will recognize those spills, now that you know what they are. Once you identify the feeling, then you can change it. Most of those negative feelings have been pre-programmed since we were little, and we go there automatically. We get triggered by certain things that "take us back." But now that you know what you know, you can replace that negative feeling, stop the oil spill, and allow yourself to reprogram your thinking. You can prevent the current potential oil spill and resulting boulder, and at the same time bust up some of those old boulders as well, resulting in feeling IN-lightened and spiritually elevated as your trash can gets emptied.

Let's look at a few examples.

1. Have you ever had a misunderstanding with your partner, spouse, or lover? Maybe you couldn't find something, and the dialogue went something like this:

    "I can't find the mustard."
    "Why are you asking me?
    Look in the refrigerator."
    "I did, but it's not where I keep it."
    "Oh, so it's *my* fault you can't find it?"

You can see where this is heading. Your partner is feeling attacked. You feel like they're not understanding you. You are not feeling any love for this person for getting defensive and causing you to get angry about it. STOP! Breathe in. Breathe out. Do it again. Instead of becoming immersed in the negative, think of two things you love about this person. Things you're grateful for. You will feel the negative feelings diminish. You have just stopped the oil spill, and your gratitude prevented another boulder from forming. Now you can also be grateful for doing that!

2. You see a homeless man holding a sign on the corner. You don't really understand how anyone could let themselves end up on the street. You are judging him. You want to tell him to go get a job. You feel yourself on edge inside. STOP! Breathe in. Breathe out. Do it again. You have no idea of this person's life. Substitute that judgment with some compassion and empathy. Smile at him. Then feel gratitude for the opportunity to see this from a different perspective so you could avoid a big spill and another boulder. Carry that gratitude feeling with you for as long as possible!

3. You have a friend and coworker that you get along with well and actually like. One day, your mutual boss chooses her for a special

assignment. You have worked there longer and would have liked that assignment. Your friend is very happy. You feel yourself pulling away from her as you fill with anger, jealousy, and envy. STOP! Breathe in. Breathe out. Do it again. This is an opportunity for you to practice compersion ~ *feeling happiness or joy because of the happiness and joy of another person*. Try it. It may be difficult but try it anyway. Try to truly experience it. Then have gratitude that you were able to ward off another spiritual spill. I promise you the feeling of gratitude will feel great, way better than the jealousy swirling in your gut.

These are just a few examples. As you become more aware, you will see that you always have an opportunity to stop a spill before it happens. And if there is no spill, there is no boulder and no mess inside your soul to clean up later. When this happens, you will be experiencing the feeling of becoming and staying IN-lightened, and that will also bring you an opportunity to feel more gratitude.

I would like to suggest that you take a few moments to reflect on this chapter and perhaps take out a piece of paper and write down a few of your personal examples where you could have stopped, taken a few breaths, and found gratitude in a given situation. I would encourage you to find at least three actual examples in your personal life as an additional exercise so that when the real deal comes along, you will be prepared ahead of time.

Still want to go deeper? As you continue your sweet spiritual journey, there are still more powerful things to include in your spiritual practice ...

CHAPTER 7

Going Deeper

*Y*ou are on the path now! You have learned where you have come from and the preprogrammed tapes you have traveled with. You also know that those don't always work, nor have they served you well. There is another way. The spiritual way. You are letting go, looking at new perspectives, opening up to the Universe, forgiving, and feeling gratitude. Awesome! By now, you should be feeling pretty wonderful and experiencing the first tastes of becoming IN-lightened! You have an understanding of your past and why you react the way you do. You are becoming more self-aware and seeking the positive perspective of every situation. You are enjoying aligning with the Universe, and you want more. Well, there is more!

Re-introducing your soul to the flow of the Universe is like meeting a new love interest. You can't get enough. And with any good relationship, you want to spend time with this reunion. I use words like re-introducing and reunion because you have always been one with the Universe deep in your soul. You are finding your way back to the pure soul you have always been. You want to grow closer in this relationship. You want to bring your best self to this relationship. You have been uncovering your best self (which has always been inside you!), and you have been learning new ways to deal with and respond to things. Now you want to go deeper. You're ready to go deeper. Okay, then! Let's look at some proven techniques to enhance your journey.

BE PRESENT/ BE MINDFUL

If I'm brooding over the past or worrying about the future, then I can't be present to what is happening right now. I can miss all the gifts that come each day. I can miss all the wonderful opportunities I have to be grateful for. I just won't notice if I'm not present. Being present means being self-aware. It means being "in the moment." It means paying attention to everything around me and my responses to those things. We all have our morning routines that, hopefully, now are beginning with your "awakening to gratitude" time.

Usually, I do awake to gratitude, but then I leap out of bed, walk to the bathroom, brush my teeth, brush my hair, get into my favorite sweats, and go downstairs to make coffee while my mind is racing through all I have to do today. How many of us just go through these events with no thought whatsoever? I decided to make it a mindful morning today. For me, it went something like this:

Awoke to gratitude.

Slowly lifted myself up to a sitting position as I noticed and thanked every muscle for making that possible.

Slowly stood up and walked to the bathroom paying attention to my feet as they rolled from heel to toe in every step, feeling gratitude for all my feet do for me.

Brushed my teeth, *slowly,* as I focused on making sure I brushed each tooth and my tongue with love, focus, and gratitude for all my teeth and tongue do for me.

Brushed my hair with love, *slowly,* and with gratitude that I have hair! I thought about how important it is in protecting my head, not just thinking about how it "looks."

I put on my favorite sweats with a different level of love and appreciation for the comfort these always bring me when I'm wearing them—more gratitude.

I *slowly* went down the stairs, taking each step one at a time as I was in awe of my legs and all they do for me each day. I thought about them; I felt them. I thanked them.

I made coffee, paying more attention to every detail of it, getting the filter, adding the water (happy to have clean water!), and expressing gratitude for whoever grew and harvested the beans. Then, as I pushed the brew button, I was grateful for a coffee pot that can make all those steps into something so wonderful.

As I waited for my coffee to brew, I felt anticipation for that first sip that was on the way as I bathed in gratitude for every little moment that brought me to this place, and I had only been up for less than 30 minutes!

I would like to strongly suggest you try this exercise! It's so amazing to me that everything can bring gratitude if we are mindful of it. This morning could have been more like a marathon, rushing through my little routine so that I could just get on with things with no thought to anything going on other than what I was trying to get to: my day, my chores, my phone calls, my bills.

What I hadn't realized was that I was already *in* my day, so why not be present, notice everything about it, and just enjoy it? My bills, chores, and responsibilities were still there, waiting for me. I would get to those, but so far, my day seemed lighter because I felt lighter. So, I decided to face everything this day with the same mindfulness. Each activity was entered into with the same focus and presence. For me, it was freeing. Even the chores felt easier to accomplish.

Please give this exercise a try and then see how long you can stay present and mindful for your entire day. See each activity as a single event, worthy of your full attention. If you like this as much as I did, you can have an entire day of mindfulness. My experience tells me that it's quite amazing, and I try to do this frequently. Any time I can be mindful and aware, whatever I am doing seems to be done with grace and ease, instead of worry and chaos!

IT HAPPENS IN THE SILENCE

I find it interesting that when we are in the womb, it's silent. We are in there for nine months of quiet. It surrounds us. It enfolds us. We just relax as we get all the nourishment and anything else we need to grow until we come into this world. Then, as we are born, we leave the silence. But it doesn't leave us. It remains inside us, there for us anytime and all the time. It's where we came from and where we need to go again to be reminded.

I actually wrote a song with this very title! I'll just share the chorus with you:

IT HAPPENS IN THE SILENCE
WHEN EVERYTHING IS QUIET.
THE UNIVERSE IS CALLING ME
CLOSER EVERY DAY.
IF I JUST STOP AND LISTEN,
I CAN ALWAYS HEAR IT.
IT HAPPENS IN THE SILENCE;
IT HAPPENS IN THE SILENCE.

If you're in a relationship, and your partner wants to talk with you, you would hopefully go sit down and give them your undivided attention. That means you wouldn't have one eye on the TV or be checking your phone every few minutes, then get up in the middle of a sentence because you just thought of something you might want to get. You know what I'm talking about!

Now you're on this amazing journey to becoming IN-lightened, and you want to have a deeper relationship with the Universe and yourself. You have to be willing to give the Universe your undivided attention as well. You must make time for it. The Universe will speak to you, but not like your partner speaks to you. The Universe speaks to you in the silence when it's quiet and still. It will speak to your heart, and you will receive answers. This is your time to go inside yourself and *hear* it. You will find that you look forward to the silence as the gift that it is.

BREATHE

Before exercise, it is recommended that you stretch and warm-up. Before any big sporting game, you will see all the players warming up. Before you go on stage to sing, you exercise your voice. Before you play a big concert, you tune your instrument. Before a presentation, you probably read over your notes or even speak the entire presentation aloud. Whatever you are getting ready to do, you will likely have some preparation so that your intention can be realized with the best possible outcome.

Since you are now learning a spiritual practice, then it stands to reason that you need to warm up here as well. You want your time with the Universe (and yourself) to be the best it can be. You wouldn't sit down and start babbling away about your problems. Perhaps you've tried that, but I don't think you came away with much satisfaction. When I spend time with the Universe, I want to be calm and relaxed. I want to stay present and feel the Universe inside of me. I want to give it my undivided attention. I want my soul to soar. The best way for me to do these things is to focus on my breath for a few minutes. There are many methods of breath control, but the one that works best for me when I'm trying to calm and focus my mind is to breathe in slowly, hold it for a few seconds, and then slowly breathe out.

As you do this, do each part of it slowly, with mindfulness. Focus on your breathing. Breathe consciously, with awareness. Feel your breath enter your nostrils and flow down into your lungs. Hold it. Then feel it leave your body with the same awareness. You can use this breathing as you go into your meditation, or you can use it anytime you feel anxious or need to just stop and become aware.

I find it interesting that the word "spirit" actually derives from the word "breath" (spiritus in Latin). And breath gives life because we can't live without it. It's important for both our bodies and minds to stay alive, but it's equally important to keep our spirits alive. So, with each breath, we need to remember who we are at the core of our being. We are Spirit, and our spirit is our soul. We can use our soul breathing to access buried emotions, grudges, and traumas (boulders!) and to release ourselves from these negative feelings. As you breathe in, you can think of everything good coming into you. Then hold that goodness inside for a few seconds. Bathe in it. Breathe out and think all of the boulders and negativity releasing their grip on you as you let go of them. Forgive them if necessary. This can be a good time to reassess some things in your life and clear out what no longer serves you.

You wash your body to keep it clean. Do your breathwork to clean your soul, tame your ego, connect to your true self, and connect to the Universe. This is another one of those things that you just need to try so you can feel it for yourself. When you do, really feel it. Experience it. Enjoy it. Be grateful that your breath is something you *can* control!

MEDITATION

Being present and mindful, breathing, and slipping into the silence are all parts of preparation for meditation. The goal is to quiet our minds so we can listen to the small voice within and have a heightened awareness in the present moment. This is when answers come. This is a very special part of your spiritual practice. This is what we have been leading to in order to go deeper.

Meditation has been practiced for thousands of years. There is nothing new about it, other than it might be new to you! There is scientific proof that meditation slows us down and causes real physiological changes like lowering our heart rate and blood pressure and raising our immunity. If we rush through our days, absorbing all the negativity around us, and never stop for a moment of silence, then it's not surprising that we might be on edge! This is the perfect opening for our egos to come out and play. When we meditate, we put the ego on hold as we come back to our beginning essence and reconnect to our wholeness and our purity. We come home.

There are so many different forms and types of meditation too numerous to mention here, but you can find them everywhere. You can meditate on your own in the silence, or you can listen to one of the wonderful guided meditations that are available. You can find many meditations and meditation experiences online for free. There is a meditation for whatever you might be dealing with. Try some, and at least one of them will resonate with you.

If you have never tried meditating before, I would suggest a guided meditation at first. It will ease you into it. They helped me in the beginning. I still enjoy a guided relaxing meditation from time to time. I like the ones that have a soothing voice guiding me, and then for the last ten or fifteen minutes, there is quiet so I can be alone with the Universe and my soul.

What's important is taking this time, treasuring this time, and making time for this time. These are special moments where you can feel one with the Universe. It's the time when you can heal the wounds of the past, let go of what no longer serves you, and plant wonderful seeds to manifest into the infinite possibilities that exist.

When I first tried to meditate, my mind was bouncing all over the place. I could sit quietly and breathe as I tried to be aware of what I was doing. But my mind had other ideas. As I read many articles about meditation, I kept trying to bring myself back. I must tell you: this was not easy. I felt frustrated because I wanted it so badly. But this cannot be rushed. If this is your spiritual practice, you will be doing it every day (or close to every day).

As with everything you practice, eventually, you will improve. Be patient with yourself. Be gentle with yourself. Try not to have expectations. Let it happen. Go inward as though you are going home ~ back to the safety and silence of the womb. Before you know it, you will get your first small glimpse of pure stillness. Perhaps it will only last a second or two, but it will be enough for you to see what's ahead. Once that happens, then you know what you are striving for. I can still remember that first time when I really felt the stillness, and my mind was completely quiet. Wow! I love that feeling!

Some believe you should set aside a special place for your meditation time, like a special chair. I think the most important thing is to be comfortable. Once you sit down, your body and mind will recognize this as meditation time. Remember, it's a practice, so practice it! Making it a practice means you are willing to show up proactively every day instead of using "crisis meditation" when things are out of control.

Try it for just fifteen minutes a day at first. And most importantly, be kind to yourself during this time.

Soon your practice will become a wonderful habit! If you begin by focusing on your breath, then every time you feel your mind wander, just go back to focusing on your breath again. It will bring you back to the stillness. I like to start with an intention, and I always try to include some gratitude. You can never have too much gratitude! Then I try to make it all about my breath and staying focused.

My meditation time takes about 30 minutes now. That gives me time to set my intention, express gratitude, and then just enjoy the time in the quiet. Since the mind has between sixty to eighty thousand thoughts a day, I know my mind will wander. Yours will too! That's okay. I just notice, then go back to my breathwork.

I prefer to start my day with meditation, then I can "reset" my soul each morning, which seems to stay with me for the day. As I said, at the beginning of my meditations, I try to set an intention. If I'm trying to manifest something, I include that right after my intention. At the end of each morning meditation, I like to speak an affirmation. Let's take a closer look at all these elements.

INTENTIONS

An intention is something you want to align with in your life. It's like an aim, purpose, or attitude you want to commit to. It can be a clear and specific wish. It's not exactly a goal you can attach expectations to or evaluate yourself on (like I want my sales to increase by

50 percent). Intentions should come from your heart, and in so doing, they can evoke feelings and purpose (like striving to be more compassionate).

Think about where you want to go with your meditation. What would you like to gain from it? What might you want to achieve? What does your heart desire? Today you might want to gain more clarity about a particular thing going on in your life right now. Or maybe it's to gain insight into something. Perhaps you are looking for a resolution to an issue in your life. It can be about your state of mind or a step towards something. You can also set the stage for your manifesting work (more about that in a minute!).

Today, my intention was to gain clarity about the journey to becoming IN-lightened and to be guided and directed to find the right words to write.

Perhaps you have a relationship issue at work or home, and you would like to approach someone with more kindness. Whatever your intention, gently invite your intention in. Don't try to force it! We are all guilty of trying to control every aspect of our lives. Setting intentions can be a powerful tool, but we must respect the process. We set the intention, or state our desire, then let go, surrender, and leave the details to the Universe! Be open to unlimited possibilities. I think it's best to keep it positive.

For example, instead of saying, "I don't want to be afraid," say, "I intend to let go of fear." I suggest you stay with an intention for a few days or a week, so you're not jumping around every day. It's also important to remember that you can't set an intention that you don't believe in. Try to make it about something you are working on right now in your life. If you can focus your mind on a specific intention during your meditation, you can bring it *into* your focused mind, thoughts, and heart. This can and will help you bring it into your reality.

And one tip a good friend shared with me is that when I'm asking the Universe to bring me something that I want, it's a good idea to ask for "this or something better." Sometimes the Universe has other bigger plans and gifts for us than we could have ever imagined. We plant the seed and then let the Universe nurture it to fruition!

Here are a few examples of intentions:

I intend to:
- Find balance.
- Open my heart and mind.
- Stay steady, calm, and focused.
- Find acceptance and forgiveness for myself and others.
- Give and receive love to myself and others.
- Let go of fear.
- Attract success and abundance.
- See the good around me.
- Be kind to myself.
- Take nothing personally.

If you have trouble thinking of your intentions, you can ask the following questions to get started:

- What matters to you most?
- What would you like to create or nurture in your life?
- What would you like to let go of or forgive in your life?
- What qualities would you like to see and cultivate in yourself?
- What are your dreams?

You may have been raised in a traditional religious home. You learned to pray to God as though God is separate from you and outside of you. Maybe you saw God as someone on a throne in the sky. Some ask for gifts as though God is Santa Claus, and if we're good, we can get those gifts. I'm suggesting another way. In staying with the premise that God/Universe is inside all of us, we don't have to pray to something outside. Remember that everything we need is inside us and always has been. We came into this world fully loaded. Trust that it's there for you because it is. Instead of begging and pleading with something way "out there," I'm suggesting a more positive type of prayer.

If we believe that everything happens in our best interest and for our highest good, then the Universe will guide and direct us. It is that small voice within that you can hear when you are in the silence. The answers will and do come. If you can think it and believe it, it can happen. The possibilities are limitless as long as your thinking is "right." We all have many false and limiting beliefs that we picked up and totally accepted through the years. It's these false and limiting beliefs that need to be overcome. We can start by replacing them with positive new beliefs, and this process flourishes in meditation.

I'd like to share my meditation practice with you. That's not to say this is the only way. You will have your own meditation, but I liked reading what others had experienced when I first started. It's just an example, not a doctrine!

I get comfortable and try to center myself. I take a few deep breaths and think of my intention for the day. After I have stated my intention, I begin my breathwork. As I breathe in, I imagine filling myself with everything good, including my gratitude and intention. If I'm trying to manifest something, I will breathe this in as well. As I hold it, I imagine it filling every cell in my body. As I breathe out, I release anything that doesn't serve me at this time and any limiting beliefs that might hold me back from reaching my intention.

Yes, my mind wanders sometimes, but I am gentle with myself and just bring myself back to my breath. I have moments of silence and quiet when I'm in the sweet spot, and those are the moments I strive for, but again, I can't force it. It just happens, and when it does, I welcome it, appreciate it, love it, and feel glorious gratitude for it. So, for me, prayer is setting my intention and asking for what I need or desire. The silence is the time to be listening for the answers. They will come. At the end of every meditation, I speak an affirmation.

Later in the afternoon or early evening, I like to do a second meditation. I do this just to release, let go, and forgive anything that has not served me this day. I never want to carry that over to the next day. I find that my sleep is more restful when I do a release meditation. My intention may be just to release, or it may include an intention specific to what I am releasing that day. Sometimes, something personal to me, my past, or an old hurt comes up, so I will work on releasing that, and my forgiveness will be for me as well as others.

Remember your meditations are personal for you. They can be whatever you need them to be. It's just between you and the wonderful Universe. Exactly how you do it is not as important as just doing it! Keep doing it until your practice becomes a habit. I promise you it will get easier with time, and you will look forward to your special time with Spirit.

AFFIRMATIONS

Spiritual affirmations are declarations to ourselves and the Universe of our intentions to make something true. They help you gently replace the negative thoughts in your head with positive thoughts, and these positive thoughts will remind you of who you are. Of course, your intention is key to the effectiveness of your affirmations. So, for me today, I intended to get more clarity regarding my book. I opened up to receive during my meditation. Then my affirmation was, "I have complete clarity in my thoughts. The right and perfect words are coming to me now." I spoke it with certainty and conviction. I said it more than once.

My preference is to end my meditation with an affirmation for my day. However, there is no right or wrong way to do this. This is your meditation! You can do affirmations before you meditate or anytime during your spiritual time. In fact, you can repeat them anytime during the day. Determine what kind of transformation you want to bring about in yourself. That would be your goal or intention. Or determine what quality, attitude, value, or characteristic you want to remind yourself of or develop in yourself. You can add an emotion as well. And, of course, gratitude is always good to offer in advance. Make your affirmations positive.

For example, if you're having a health issue, say, "I am healthy and whole," or "Healing energy is flowing through me now." Say it as though it is so. Some say it takes twenty-one days of repetition for an affirmation to make its mark on your psyche (just like some say it takes twenty-one days to make a habit), so try to keep your affirmation going for at least a month.

In the beginning, you will have to consciously choose to repeat your spiritual affirmations. The more you repeat them, the sooner they will begin to replace the negative mind chatter that takes over when we're not monitoring our thoughts.

You will want to create your own personal affirmations, but here are a few examples to get you started!

- I am healthy and whole.
- I easily see the lesson or the blessing in all that is.

- Every day, I offer gratitude, trust, and faith for everything that happens in my life.
- I am authentic and present.
- I am successful in everything I attempt.
- I am a magnet for money and abundance.
- When faced with two choices, I always take the higher path.
- I am guided by a higher power that is inside me and all around me.
- Divine order is at work in my life.
- I am open and receptive to the good the Universe has for me.

One more thing needs to be mentioned here. Remember, we are affirming what we already know is true at the soul level. We probably have had lots of old programming that can pop up, creating doubt and limiting beliefs. But inside, in your purest form, you already have all that you are asking for! Faith or belief is the key when speaking affirmations. Your thoughts are powerful. If you really have doubt, then you are just going through the motion of the affirmation process. See it happening. Feel it. Know it. Believe that it can and will happen. Then let the Universe do the rest!

MANIFEST YOUR DESTINY

Manifesting is about turning your dreams into reality. It's about bringing something tangible into your life through attraction and belief. Your thoughts are powerful, and if you think it, you can make it happen.

But it's not just positive thinking that will bring you what you want. You don't just make a wish, and it magically comes true. You still must take proactive steps in the direction of your desires. You need your thoughts, actions, beliefs, and emotions on board as well!

The first step to manifesting is knowing exactly what you want. For example, it's not enough to just say, "I want to find a mate." Be specific about the qualities and characteristics that you want in *your* mate. The clearer and more concise you can be, the better. Think about exactly what your hopes, dreams, and goals are. Obviously, if you don't know exactly what you want, you won't be able to relay that to the Universe. How can you expect to manifest your dreams if you don't have a clear picture of what those dreams are?

Think about what your life will look like once you do have your dream. Think about how it will feel. Try to actually feel that feeling. Picture yourself living your dream as if it's already yours. If it helps you get clarity, write your dream and all its elements on paper. Read it over and over. Focus on it. Think about it. Breathe it in. If you have difficulty seeing and knowing your dreams, meditation is a powerful tool that will give you the space to clear your mind so you can find the clarity you need to manifest.

Some people like to journal about it or create a vision board. Remember, you are going to live as though you already have what you want. (Don't forget to be grateful for it!) Maybe you want more abundance, a new and fulfilling career, or better health. The procedure is the same as it would be for finding your perfect mate.

When you are crystal clear, then you can ask the Universe for what you want. Once you've asked for what you want, you are not finished. A magic fairy will not appear with your dream mate or dream job! You still have to continue to believe it to be so. And you need to take action. Start being the person who already has, does, and feels your dreams and desires. Use visualization to see yourself with whatever you want to manifest.

Check in on your beliefs that might be inhibiting your progress of finding your perfect mate ("I'm not good enough," "Relationships never work."), or the perfect job ("I'm not smart enough," "I could never earn that much money."). If you have a health issue, see yourself as the perfect whole and healthy being you *are*. Do not own your disease. It is not you!

You probably have years of preprogrammed thoughts and beliefs that may hold you back. Try to identify these. Replace those limiting beliefs by using affirmations to change your thinking. Try to remember how powerful your mind is. If you think it, it can happen. You can dream big. You can create your own reality. The possibilities are endless!

MEDITATION TOOLBOX

We have gone over the basics of how meditation can help you clear your path to Spirituality. You will begin to see and feel the difference for yourself. By becoming IN-lightened, you will be releasing all of your old, limited thoughts and preprogramming. In their place, you will fill yourself with positive thoughts and feelings. You will substitute negative reactions with loving, compassionate responses. As you continue your journey and include meditation in your daily practice, you may want to try some of the other "tools" that are available.

Feeling Substitution

If you want to specifically work on substituting an "old" feeling for a "new" positive one, try the following:

- Get relaxed as you do for your meditation.
- Take a few deep breaths, and then, on your next inhale, you will breathe in the feeling you want to feel.
- On the exhale, you will release the negative feeling that can hold you back.

You can work on just one of these and repeat it several times or work on a few of them. Choose the feelings that you want to work on most for this meditation. Perhaps you have set an intention to be more accepting. So, for this, you would breathe in acceptance on your inhale, and on your exhale, release judgment.

Here is a sample list of some of the feelings you might want to work on:

INHALE	**EXHALE/RELEASE**
Acceptance	Judgment
Tolerance	Anger
Love	Fear
Forgiveness	Revenge
Faith	Doubt
Trust	Anxiety
Strength	Fragility
Soothing	Pain
Peace	Chaos

There are many more, but this is a great meditation tool to keep in your toolbox whenever you need it! You can use this exercise anytime during the day if you feel one of those boulder-building emotions.

Mantras

Some people like to use mantras. A mantra is a word or sound that is repeated to aid in your concentration during your meditation. You've probably already heard of "Om." There are many mantras to choose from. You can find a mantra for just about anything you want to focus on, from self-love, good health, and confidence to gratitude and peace, etc. Many people find that using a mantra can boost awareness and improve concentration. This is another one of those things that you just need to try and see how you feel. If you can stay focused on just your breathwork, then you might not need a mantra, but you'll have to see for yourself. It's always in your toolbox should you need it.

The TAB Technique

This technique was created by Rev. Charles Roth. The TAB stands for Totally Accept the Belief. It's our limiting beliefs and early programming that hold us back from manifesting our dreams and desires. It's great to write our dreams down and speak them, but if we don't truly believe them, we will just be going through the motions and wondering why our dreams are not being fulfilled. For example, let's say you want to buy a house, but your "old" belief system tells you that you will never make enough money to afford it. This is a limiting belief that you are not good enough. You need to write down something like this:

I totally accept the belief that the Universe is guiding me, and all things are working together so that the right and perfect house will be mine. I am grateful.

Notice that it begins with "I *totally* accept the belief." That leaves no room for doubt or worry. And, of course, you want to be grateful for what is coming and behave as if it's already here. This is a wonderful type of affirmation. Write it down. Say it three times with concentrated attention, then release it from your mind completely. Go about doing whatever is next in your life. The "seed belief" will be working. The next time you have worry or concern about this, again, take out your TAB and repeat it three times. Say it without any strain or effort to try to make it true. Be gentle and just *know*. Surrender to the Universe!

Rituals

Many people like to include some sort of ritual for their spiritual time. That would include doing it at the same time every day, adding incense, music, a special area of the house, or sitting in the same chair just for your meditation. These are not necessary, but for some, they help set the mood. These extras are available if you want to try them and see how they work for you.

I like to think of my entire meditation time as a ritual for my day. I have tried incense, music, and even fragrant candles to enhance my meditation. I'm partial to candles and soft spa-like music, but I will tell you that once I'm deep into my meditation, I barely notice any of those outside elements! The key is to set a relaxing mood. If you're not sure what that might be, then I suggest you try them all to see how you feel about them. Remember, it's always about what works best for *you*!

Angels and Guides

If you are so inclined, you can feel free to call in spirit guides and angels into your meditation. This can include lost loved ones. I sometimes call my daughter, Holland. No amount of manifesting will bring her back into this dimension, but I can hold her close in a meditation. For those of you in grief, you might want to try this. Picture their face; look into their eyes. Feel them around you. I can't say for sure that my daughter joins me, but I can tell you that I have felt her many times. It usually comes with a good cry, and I mean that. It's a *good* cry. There is a Buddhist saying I just love:

"When someone you love dies, nothing changes.
Everything is the same.
The only difference is that they are not outside of you."

So, if they are no longer outside of you, then they must be inside of you. That thought in itself has helped me so much. If you want to look more into angels and guides, much is written about it. I just wanted to give you a few more of the possibilities available for your toolbox should you want to go further. You will find what is comfortable for you, and those are the tools you should use. You certainly don't have to use them all.

Remember, meditation is a magnificent tool! You can set the entire tone of your day by beginning with meditation. You will find that you also make better decisions from the meditative state. There are many books and resources on all aspects of meditation should you want to read more and learn more. And there are volumes of information on the internet for free as well as wonderful guided meditations, mantras, and more.

I hope that meditation will be a regular part of your daily practice as you are becoming IN-lightened and clearing your path to Spirituality. Like any path, it's not always smooth. You have years of negative programming and a load of boulders to crush! Just be gentle with yourself. You are participating in a life-changing journey. Once you surrender, you will enter the unbelievable realm of infinite possibilities. Like in any endeavor, practice, or undertaking, there is a learning curve, and there can be setbacks and pitfalls. That doesn't mean you are doing anything wrong. You are doing everything right! Don't get discouraged. You are on the right path. Keep doing it! Let's look at some of the pitfalls that may show up, so that if they appear, you can be aware and ready to take action!

CHAPTER 8

Pitfalls on the Path

*Y*ou are further down the path now (or I should say *up* the path!). You are emptying your trash can a little more each day. You feel like you are in the flow. By now, I hope you are realizing that life is meant to be an exciting, joyful, creative learning experience. And even with all we have learned, and all of the boulders we have crushed and removed, we will still have challenges. It's just the way of the world. But we need to remember that God/the Universe does not give us these challenges. It's just what happens ... to all of us.

What's important is how we react and respond to those challenges. Our challenges may be financial, personal, or professional. You may think that this spiritual journey is not easy sometimes, but neither is carrying around a load of boulders and negativity! And even with all we have learned and practiced, you still may encounter a big bump in the road, which can open up some spiritual pitfalls that we all can face.

FEAR

We learned that fear is one of the big spiritual oil spills, but it's also one of the pitfalls on the path, and it's a big pitfall for all of us. This stands to reason because it's one of those learned behaviors (old habits) that would be one of the first to crop up. You know that feeling in the pit of your stomach when you feel fear. We can feel it anytime a challenge presents itself—fear over a financial challenge, a health issue, or a personal relationship problem. And once the fear grabs hold, we tend to want to control it. Remember that fear is triggered by the *perception* of danger, real or imagined. It makes us want to *do* something to stop it. Instead, ask yourself, "Who am I willing to *be* in the face of this? … Not "What can I *do*?"

If you have been directed by fear most of your life, then anxiety is nothing new to you. We can actually become addicted to fear and negativity. So, you might be making great progress on your spiritual path while things are going well, but familiar fear may also pop up as soon as a big challenge presents itself. This is a spiritual pitfall. If we get consumed by it, we may also develop doubts that our new ways just aren't working. This is not true!

With each challenge, you will have to focus on what you now know to be true. And one truth we have learned is that what will impede your work of becoming IN-lightened more than anything is your paralyzing, fearful thoughts, which are fed by your limiting beliefs. Stop! You can control your thoughts. You can replace your thoughts. You can't stop your thoughts from coming; they are popping into your mind all day long. However, you can replace them so that they don't cause a spiritual oil spill.

Begin with a slow deep breath. Relax and then pull from your new arsenal of emotions.

EGO

I must mention ego. We all have one. Some are more active than others! There is nothing wrong with having an ego. It actually serves to protect us, but it does need to be regulated. When we are born, we are pure Spirit, and our souls are the true reflection of that spirit. But as we move through this human world, the soul becomes identified with the body, and that's when the ego comes alive. In this world, for most of us, the ego is the guiding principle of all thoughts. When left unregulated, it affects your decision-making, your mood, and gives you justification for your behavior.

We are becoming IN-lightened to rid ourselves of all the negativity, traumas, and hurts we have built up. In that process, we will also be regulating our egos. So, with every challenge that comes, we now need to look at them from the soul level. The ego will *react*, but the soul will *respond*. For instance, just the other day, I called a friend of mine. She was impatient and acted like my call was an inconvenience (from my perspective). My ego jumped right in with indignance: "She can't talk to me like that." In the past, I might not have answered her calls for weeks because my ego was so involved. Today, after becoming IN-lightened, my ego tried, but I was able to stop, breathe and then feel compassion for what she might have been dealing with at the time of the phone call. I changed an ego reaction to a soul response. I felt so much better. The less reactive and more responsive we can be, the more spiritual we will become.

And the more spiritual we are, the easier it will be to respond to any situation. You have many opportunities each day to either react or respond. Notice what is happening and be aware of how you are showing up with all these small instances each day. Then when a larger challenge arises, you will be familiar with all options, and choosing the soul path will happen more easily. Reacting with your ego is a pitfall you want to avoid!

IGNORING THE LAW OF ATTRACTION

Simply put, the law of attraction is a philosophy suggesting that positive thoughts bring positive results into a person's life, while negative thoughts bring negative results. We have already determined how powerful our thoughts are. So, it follows that negative thinking will attract negative experiences, and positive thinking will attract positive experiences. If we remove negative thoughts and things from our lives and replace them with positive ones, our lives will be better and happier.

At any given moment, we can feel like the present is somehow less than we want. Instead, we need to focus our energies on finding ways to make the present moment the best it can be. Choose to see the good. Can you think of a situation in your life right now that you have negative thoughts about? Take my example in the previous section, where I mentioned calling my impatient friend. Instead of letting my ego feel those negative emotions, I chose to have compassion for whatever her situation might have been. Try looking at your situation from a different perspective and find a positive in it. Feel that change of thought. Know that good is on the way. You will be attracting it with your change of thought. And it's always wonderful to take these moments to find something to be grateful for. I'm grateful she is my friend, and a moment of impatience doesn't change that. Remember how wonderful gratitude *always* feels, and there is always something we can be grateful for at every moment.

HOLDING A GRUDGE

So now you know all about forgiveness and letting go of grudges you had before you began your journey to IN-lightenment. You probably even tried practicing forgiveness for others and yourself. Now that you are on the path, here comes a situation, say in your workplace. A coworker has done something that has really affected you negatively. Maybe they even apologized for it. But every day, you have to see this person, and you just can't shake how you feel. Stop. Take a good look at the situation. Are you reacting with your disgruntled ego? You don't like feeling this way, but every morning when you come into the office, you are reminded, and you still feel like you're "not ready" to forgive or let go. This hurts you. This hurts your soul. Think about how your soul would respond, not how your ego would react. This is a pitfall that can set you back.

Perhaps a forgiveness meditation is in order. You are the captain of your ship. Once you are on the path, crushing your boulders and emptying your trash can, you certainly don't want to put new boulders in their place. Take the forgiveness route, and then you can feel gratitude that you did!

RESISTANCE

Another big pitfall is resistance. Things aren't going exactly as you want them to. This is when you need to open up to the Universe and all the possibilities that are working for you, whether you can see them or not. Trying to force and control things hasn't worked so far, and it's not going to work this time either. When you're in the flow, the movement is fluid and easy. When you are resisting, things are rigid and tight. This is the perfect opportunity to practice acceptance of the situation along with the certainty that the Universe is handling it. Trust that.

I'd like to share a story with you about a friend of mine who was a truck driver. She still had children at home and constantly felt guilty about being gone all the time. She judged herself, and others judged her as a mom for not being home, but she couldn't afford to work for minimum wage, and truck driving paid very well. After she got most of her debts paid off, she still didn't quit that job. She resisted change because truck driving was what she knew, even though it came with judgment and guilt, two big oil spills. Later, she lost her job when the pandemic hit. By then, no one was hiring. She was forced to get creative to find something to do. She finally accepted being home (because she was forced to) and found a career in editing. She built it into a successful business at home, and now everyone is happy. On top of that, she enjoys what she's doing. No more guilt and judgment. God/the Universe knew what was best for her (as usual!!). Once she accepted the change of being home, she opened up to a new opportunity that otherwise would never have presented itself.

Go back to your spiritual truths and know that everything happens for our highest good, even when we can't see it. This also goes for disappointment that comes your way. Don't push or try to control the situation. Accept and realize that God/the Universe is in control. When you feel the negative energy that comes with resistance, stop. Accept that this is happening. With acceptance comes peace. Know that it will change. You might not know right at this moment, but it will come. You don't need to know every little detail. God knows! Surrender to it. It's working for you.

GRIEF

This one is difficult. I know it all too well. Losing a loved one is not easy. Especially when you lose a child. There is nothing that can take away grief. I actually think it's a natural process that we have to go through. If we don't embrace the grief and let it happen, that in itself can create another boulder. The Universe can't help in the actual grief process, but where it does and will help is in managing the resulting negative emotions we choose to feel when we are grieving, such as anger, resentment, blame, guilt, and more.

You're going to miss your loved one, and grieving is okay. It takes time. But we certainly don't have to fall into the trash can along with all our boulders. Those accompanying negative reactions will only take you further away from what you are trying to accomplish here. And none of those horrible reactions will bring your loved one back. My daughter died in 2013. I still have moments of deep grief. One thing I realized is that I'm crying for myself because I miss her. So, I let myself have a good cry and then try to think of something to be grateful for regarding my life with her in it. And I'm always grateful for my memory that allows me to remember the beautiful moments.

BEING A VICTIM

Being a victim is a gift to your ego. It allows your ego to really come out and play as it asks, "Why me?"

And egos love the pity parties that result. Remember, why is not a question that can be answered to your satisfaction. The answer to why is always "because it is." And here's a why question for you ... Why do we ask "why" when something "bad" happens, but we don't ask "why" when something good happens? Life happens. Challenges happen. We can't avoid them. When we fight this, we can easily become a victim. We don't need to understand everything that happens. We can't.

Don't let yourself be held hostage by the past. Try to focus on acceptance. This is when we can practice regulating our overactive ego that will enjoy telling you that you are justified in being angry, resentful, or judgmental. But ego gratification is temporary and never satisfied. You can control your thoughts, but can you control your ego? It wants to feel angry, resentful, victimized, defensive, and all of the negative human emotions we wallow in. While you are on this amazing path, try to put your ego on a "diet" for a while as you fill your soul with the positive. There is no ego in your soul.

Try to respond to the situation at hand with loving kindness, acceptance, and compassion. That's your soul. If you're reacting, then that's your ego. It's okay to press "reset" and change from a reaction (your ego) to a response (your soul). If you look hard enough, you can always find a positive (even when your ego doesn't want to because it's having so much fun at the pity party). And don't forget to look for something to be grateful for. I'm not saying this is always easy. It's not, but remember, this is a "practice," ~ so practice it! Change being a victim to being a victor!

I NEED FIXING

Another thing the ego loves is to tell you that you need fixing. But the truth is that there is nothing to fix at all. We only need to fix broken things, and you are not broken! Someone in your past may have convinced you that you were broken, but that is a limiting belief. The truth is that you are perfect and whole. You have everything you need. It's there now as it always has been. You just need to tap into it. Choose a response instead of a reaction.

This path is a process of waking up to the truth and changing our perception so that we see that we are already perfect as we are right now. Nothing is missing. We need to be mindful of this as we stay present. I believe that presence is the way to freedom.

If you are being mindful, you will notice your familiar stories of fear and lack. You can refuse to interact with those stories. Replace them with knowing the truth of who you really are. Life includes some pain and challenges, but those pains and challenges are not who we are. Do not be defined by labels. If we get caught in ego and fear, then we might think there is something wrong with us. Stop.

As humans, life is sometimes messy for everyone. The work of loving and healing yourself as you remove your boulders means staying present and holding all parts of your experience with love and compassion. So, if you see yourself reacting to a situation with anger or judgment, think of a soul response to respond with instead. It's there for you. You are safe.

I CAN'T TAKE NO FOR AN ANSWER

Another pitfall is thinking that every prayer should be answered the way *you* want it to be answered. Sometimes "no" is the answer to your prayer. It's wonderful to know what you want and to be able to ask God/the Universe for it. But it's also wonderful if you can learn to accept the wisdom of the Universe gracefully. Not being able to take no for an answer is a pitfall that can cause you to lose trust in the process and make you want to give up your journey. You are not in control here. Express your desires to the Universe and trust that you will get exactly what you need, even if it's not exactly the way you perceived it happening. We don't have a crystal ball and we can't see the future, but we can stay present and know that everything will work out for our highest good. There should be comfort in that thought, no matter what you are wishing for.

Remember, we don't know the entire plan. We only know that the Universe is working for us ... always.

INACTION

Thinking it, wanting it, then not taking any action can be another big pitfall. What are you waiting for?

Waiting for the "right" moment when everything seems easy might just be waiting too long. Although sometimes it can be easy and effortless, this is not always the case. Waiting, without any action on our part, can actually be a kind of resistance that will keep you stuck.

So, when you find yourself in the waiting game, take another look and take action. Be a partner with the Universe in making things happen. That doesn't mean to force things, but rather embrace the attitude that the right time is now. You still want to have positive thoughts and see yourself as a magnet for your desires. For instance, if you want a new job or career, you can make it your intention, and then you could just sit and wait, or you could take steps to create it now by going on interviews and networking. You can participate in your manifestation.

Remember Spiritual Truth #4: *When you move with the Universe, it moves with you, through you, and for you.*

PUTTING HUMAN RESPONSIBILITIES AHEAD OF YOUR SPIRITUAL PRACTICE

We all have busy lives. There will be a time when the temptation to skip your morning meditation will happen. It will be to take care of something "more pressing." But that one day can turn into two days and then into a week. Stress will build up again as you move away from your spiritual path and slip back more into the "human" world. It's easy to do. I know. I have done it myself.

And as I let myself get further away from my spiritual practice, I noticed that the everyday stresses began to affect me more as I found it easier to slip back into my reactions and further away from responding with my soul. And I have actually felt disconnected from Spirit. Don't worry if this happens. Be gentle with yourself. You are always connected—all the time. You just have to dial back in. I found that when I put my spiritual practice behind my "real" life, it was actually when I needed that practice the most! If this happens to you, just know you have done nothing wrong, and you are still everything you need to be.

Simply and gently make time for your spiritual practice the next day (or even this day!). And when you do, notice those first few breaths and how amazing they feel. Be grateful you found your way back. The reason for making your spiritual time a priority is that when you show up every day, you are able to deal with whatever comes in a more graceful and soulful way. It helps give your day the best start possible. Occasionally, even now, I might miss a day, but I try never to miss more than one. I now know the benefits of having a spiritual practice, and I look forward to it and all the goodness that comes with it. You will too.

GIVING UP TOO SOON

One of the biggest pitfalls, especially when you are new to this journey, is giving up too soon. You started this journey; I'm assuming because your life wasn't exactly the way you wanted in every area. You knew there was more, or something you were missing (the Universe!), so you were seeking. But like many of us, we are impatient. We want instant gratification and quick results. Maybe you're having trouble being still because it's unfamiliar to you. Maybe no one else you know is doing this and doesn't understand why you are. Maybe you haven't "felt" the Spirit yet. Perhaps you thought you would be instantly happy and no more challenges would come your way.

Seeking perpetual happiness and being disappointed if there is a moment of unhappiness can cause you to think of giving up. Don't! Remember, you will still have challenges. We all do. We need to accommodate them. Problems are not personal … It's just life! And you can have peace of mind no matter what is showing up in your life.

Remember that things happen around you and in you, but what matters most is what happens *to* you. It's how you show up! The problems and challenges are actually gifts and opportunities for growth. Stay with it. Show up every day for a few months, and then see how you feel. By that time, you will have had many instances of pure joy with your journey despite any challenges that come your way. Once you know … you know. But if you stop too soon, you'll never know!

CHAPTER 9

Moving Forward

*O*nce you have identified and purged your spiritual oil spills and boulders, you will feel like a soaring hot air balloon. You will feel light and free and at peace. You will be able to connect with the Universe and everyone in it. You will feel Spirit with you wherever you go. You will notice your many blessings and feel the joy of gratitude. You will be in the flow.

Now that you have all the tools to become IN-lightened and want to clear your path to Spirituality, you may be wondering just how to get started, what to expect, and what to remember.

Let's take a look at those things.

GETTING STARTED

There is no time like the present to get started! Think of this as the amazing journey it is to discover your true inner self. Your perfect, pure, clean soul awaits your rediscovery! It's always been there, but circumstances, a lifetime of preprogrammed limiting beliefs, and negative self-talk have gotten in the way and created so many boulders that you may not even be sure it's there anymore. But it is. Think of it as going home, and as you uncover your sweet soul, you will love what you find. You will want to nourish it and care for it. The rewards are endless.

All you need to do is take that first step into the silence to be with your soul and the Universe. Try your first meditation today. Give it to yourself as the gift that it is. Make a commitment to yourself to try it for one month. Give your morning meditation your first attention of each day. And try to fit in that second meditation in the late afternoon as well. Begin slowly, even if you try it for only five minutes the first time. Try all the different things in your toolbox and see which ones work best for you. Try a gratitude exercise. Remember, there is a free journal for you to download on my website as a guide: DeniseGanulin.com.

Begin being mindful and present to how you react. Look at where those reactions may have come from and what boulders were created as a result. Then, you can make your intention to let go of those old feelings and beliefs as you crush the boulders that go with them. Free yourself and your amazing soul.

There is something called the Law of Diminishing Intent. It states that the longer we delay doing something, the less likely we will do it. You have taken the first step by reading this book. But like we have learned, now you have to take action. Why put it off? There is so much good waiting for you!

NURTURE YOURSELF

You will be rediscovering your soul and your best self. It's time to think about you and how you can care for yourself. Think about the things that make you happy and lovingly give those things to yourself. If a potential challenge presents itself, and you feel some of those old ways stirring, then do something that makes you feel good at your soul level and remind yourself of who you are.

For example, here are a few things that I like to do for myself that make me and my soul happy. These might interest you as well, but feel free to make your own list!

Take a walk outdoors with nature.	Listen to music that I love.
Dance to the music I love.	Look at the ocean.
Take a hot bubble bath.	Laugh.
Play with my grandchildren.	Do a meditation.

Call a friend.	Do something nice for someone else.
Volunteer to serve others.	Think of three things I'm grateful for right now.

Or try this: on an afternoon when the weather is nice, try canceling any and all obligations for the rest of the day. Do whatever makes you happy with no time constraints. Look through new eyes like you are seeing and doing these things for the first time. Go without expectations and see where the day takes you. Smile!

COMMIT TO YOUR PRACTICE

Make your spiritual practice your priority. Give it your time and attention. Do your meditation. Do your gratitude work. Read and listen to the amazing material out there that will make you feel even more connected to the Universe. One thing that I love to think of is that I am not separate from the Universe. I am not *in* the Universe. The Universe is *in* me!!

I treasure that. I want to spend time there. You will, too, once you let yourself surrender to the journey and take that first step. Know, experience, and love the silence. That's where peace and the answers will come. Always remember that you are a perfect expression of all you seek to be. You are perfect yet evolving in that perfection. This journey is about becoming more aware of everything you already are!

REMEMBER WHAT YOU KNOW

We have learned all about the negative reactions that we have used for so long and the positive replacement responses to use instead. Yes, there will still be challenges, but soon you might find yourself saying, "Oh yes, this is anger ... I can do this one!" Lean into the challenge and look for the message in every problem. Ask, "What is here in this problem for me to learn, and what do I want to be in the face of it?" Go into the silence and let your soul speak to you. Begin paying attention to life and know that life is speaking to you all the time. Be grateful for the lessons.

You know about the Law of Attraction. It's a good one to remember if a negative thought creeps into your head. You are now equipped to find an alternative response that will give you a much better result. The more positivity you put out into the world, the more positivity you will bring into your life. Your thoughts are so powerful. And now you have so many tools to help you bring so much goodness into your life.

One of my favorite quotes from Buddha is:

"What you think you become.
What you feel you attract.
What you imagine you create."

Welcome to the world of infinite possibilities!

WHAT YOU CAN EXPECT

As you clear your path to Spirituality, here are just a few things you can expect to notice:

More:	Less:
Clarity	Anxiety
Confidence	Self-doubt
Personal growth	Fear
Happiness	Judgment
Inner peace	Worry
Kindness	Anger
Love	Resentment
Appreciation	Negativity
Joy	Sadness
Faith	Doubt
Intuition	Insecurity
Freedom	Constriction
Truth	Limiting beliefs
Gratitude	Victimhood

HOW DO I KNOW I'M ON THE RIGHT TRACK?

Over time you will notice the wonderful changes and transformations that are occurring. It's natural to wonder if you're on the right track. There is a story about a disciple who once asked the Buddha how he would know the truth if he found it. The Buddha answered, "You know the truth because the truth works." So too, will you know you are on the right path because it works! Your life will work better. The first time you consciously choose peace over chaos or knowingly respond to a situation instead of reacting to it, you will be in the flow—time to notice every gift from the Universe as a sign that you are on the right track.

A sign of progress is when you find that you have stopped fighting the nature of life. Instead, you are working with it. Another sign is when you notice that you have stopped pretending life is supposed to be a certain way, and you begin to accept it on its own terms. You can acknowledge your limiting beliefs, substitute them with your new improved beliefs and then get on with your journey. You will find that you feel happier and more engaged in every aspect of your wonderful soul-filled life! There will always be some pain along the way. If we resist or fear the pain, then we suffer. When pain arises (and it will), try to greet it with more of a calm curiosity about the lesson to follow and the spiritual growth you will receive. And don't forget gratitude, gratitude, gratitude!

NEVER TOO LATE

No matter how old you are, what you've been through, or how low you think you've fallen, it's never too late to discover your soul and its amazing connection to the Universe. You may be so far down in your life that you just can't see a way out. Accept where you are right now and remember the light is still there whether you can see it or not at this moment. Open up and give it a try. Remember, this is a journey that will last for your entire life. There really isn't a final destination where you can stop doing the wonderful work you have been doing. This will be part of your life, your day, your experiences, and everything you do. Surrender to the Universe. It will take you on the ride of your life!

THE GIFT OF LOVE

Spirituality is the wonderful gift of love. Love for ourselves and love for others. Love for everything in this world. But the greatest love will be in your relationship with God/the Universe. We are loved … unconditionally. We can receive this unconditional love, and we can give it back out to our world. As I've said several times, we are perfect and whole just as we are. Just to *be* is a blessing. We are special creations in this Universe, which makes us extraordinary.

Faith in the perfection of the Universe (even when things are tough) can make the difference between a life of happiness and a life of bitterness. The Universe offers that sweet happiness, along with joy and love. It's always available, and the gifts are always there to find. While you're choosing more positive responses and becoming comfortable with the good emotions that go along with those responses, don't forget to treat yourself with those same wonderful emotions … forgiveness, kindness, compassion, and love. You deserve it!

A FEW FINAL THOUGHTS

You are embarking on the journey of a lifetime. An IN-lightened journey! You will be amazed at the many things you will uncover and learn as you empty your trash can of a lifetime of unwanted boulders and negative emotions that no longer serve you. You will gain more confidence in the process every day. As a spiritual person, the good work you do inside yourself will be reflected in the actions you take in every situation in your life. So keep meditating and doing your spiritual practice, and have faith. As you awaken to the truth of who you really are and see the changes taking place in your life, then the hurts, traumas, and challenges that hung over you for so long will fade into the distant past.

There is no perfect place to be reached and no final destination at the end. In fact, there is no end at all! It's all right here and now in one moment of being present after another as you find and express your own truth. You will be a beacon of light to others and enjoy giving the same unconditional love that you feel coming from the Universe.

My wish is for you to love this life and journey as you learn to fully live in an IN-lightened state. And even more, I wish you the sweet joy you will discover as you fall in love with yourself, your soul, and everything in this Universe!

"When you feel like you're at the end of your rope, make a knot and sit and swing!"

~Denise Ganulin

Thank You for Reading

Becoming
IN-LIGHTENED

If you enjoyed the practices introduced in this book and believe they will benefit others, please take a moment to write an honest review on Amazon (or wherever you purchased this book!) Every review matters, and it matters a lot!

Your input is valuable and genuinely appreciated.

Thank you so much!

Let's connect!

Email: Denise@DeniseGanulin.com

Facebook: Author Denise Ganulin

Instagram

You can find additional tools and assistance on your journey to Spiritual IN~lightenment by going to my website at DeniseGanulin.com.

Don't forget to download your free journal! Your journey to peace is truly just a step away.

Blessings,

~Denise Ganulin

ACKNOWLEDGMENTS

I'd like to thank the following people who have helped me on my journey:

My family and friends for their encouragement and support.

My angel daughter, Holland, who continues to be my muse from the other side.

Bidu and Jove, my two amazing grandchildren, who inspire me daily to learn and grow and see the world through the eyes of a child.

Gary, for loving and supporting me and allowing me all the time I need to write.

Amanda, who read each chapter as it was written and gave me honest, loving input.

All the coaches, teachers, and encouragers from Self-Publishing School who held my hand all the way.

All the people who brought less than ideal situations to my life ... thank you for the learning experiences and growth that came from each situation.

The Universe. It has taught me so much. I have so much gratitude.

ABOUT THE AUTHOR

*D*enise Ganulin has been a singer/songwriter for many years, performing her songs across the country. She writes spiritual songs, songs for grievers, and songs for soldiers … all areas close to her heart.

This is her first "self-help" book, but her second published book. Her first book was released in 2021 and is titled *Bidu's Adventures ~ Fairy Beginnings*, a fantasy chapter book for 7 to 14-year-olds. It incorporates spirituality and love, two of Denise's favorite topics! She is currently working on another fantasy chapter book called *Jove's Magical Adventures*. You can stay updated on the latest releases of her books by following her on Amazon.

Denise lost her only child, Holland, several years ago. This book is a tribute to her and all they learned together on their journey to Spirituality. Holland left behind two amazing children who fill Denise's life with joy, love, and inspiration. They are the wonderful inspiration for her children's fantasy chapter books.

You can follow Denise on Amazon, Instagram and Facebook and see samples of her books and music on her website at DeniseGanulin.com.

Made in the USA
Columbia, SC
09 May 2023